THE LAW OF TERRITORIAL WATERS OF MID-OCEAN ARCHIPELAGOS AND ARCHIPELAGIC STATES

THE LAW OF TERRITORIAL WATERS OF MID-OCEAN ARCHIPELAGOS AND ARCHIPELAGIC STATES

by

BARRY HART DUBNER

MARTINUS NIJHOFF/THE HAGUE/1976

ISBN 978-94-015-0389-1 ISBN 978-94-015-0983-1 (eBook)
DOI 10.1007/978-94-015-0983-1

FOREWORD

It is a truism that the increasingly rapid movement in technology is forcing change and shift in the norms of international law. The 149 states of the Law of the Sea Conferences of the United Nations have been attempting to establish and develop adequate legal norms that will take into account the need for the orderly growth and use of the changing technological capabilities and the resulting economic development that cannot and should not be hindered by inadequate law. When such norms are identified and agreed by a substantial majority of states, they are usually set out and placed into multilateral treaties.

The rules governing the resource and non-resource allocation of the oceans and the uses of the oceans have posed major difficulties for the development of international law for many years. The Geneva Conference of 1958 building upon the groundwork of the International Law Commission of the United Nations shaped a rough structure for a 20th Century Law of the Seas and formulated the effort in four major international conventions. But a majority of the states failed to ratify or accede to the conventions. Even had they become effective as the expression of the Law of the Seas in the second half of the 20th Century, there was one glaring area of omission: a conventional law for the waters of mid-ocean archipelagos and archipelagic states.

Professor Dubner's work is a painstaking effort to analyze the archipelago problems as lacunae in the law. He begins his analysis from the two polarized positions of (a) the traditional maritime nations and (b) the self-proclaimed archipelagic states. After setting forth a discussion of the related norms of the traditional laws of the sea, he turns to an acute discussion of the geographical and legal limitations that confront the general maritime nations and archipelagic states when pressing their respective declarations and claims. Professor Dubner's proposal is unique in that it proposes that each group surrender certain sovereign rights hitherto recognized in international law in order to reach a satisfactory compromise. Professor Dubner realistically takes into consideration the very distinct probability that the states, whether as a product of the Law of the Sea Conferences or not, will be adopting a 12-mile territorial waters limit and a 200-mile exclusive economic zone. The complications of this probability for his archipelagic state proposals are fully recognized. He thereafter sets forth "extreme" examples of how his *indicator formula* proposal would actually be applied to archipelagic areas such as the thousands of islands scattered over thousands of miles of Micronesia on the one hand and the one large island and immediately adjacent smaller islands of the Republic of Ireland. Other in between archipelagic state situations are also discussed.

The study can be recommended to students and practitioners who are concerned with the evolution of the law of the sea, and to those who are interested in inventive suggestions to modify traditional norms in this difficult area of the law.

ALBERT H. GARRETSON

ACKNOWLEDGMENTS

This work is dedicated to my beloved father, PAUL PEPPE DUBNER, to my beloved brother, HOWARD EVERETT DUBNER, and to my mother, PRISCILLA HART DUBNER.

I wish to express my warmest love and affection to my wife, Bonnie, for her encouragement and assistance throughout this period of our lives.

A special expression of gratitude is extended to my Research Advisor, Professor Albert H. Garretson and to the other members of the Thesis Committee, Professors Andreas F. Lowenfeld and Stanley N. Futterman.

Throughout the research and writing of this work every effort has been made to reflect the implications of a concept of "symbiosis" and, in particular, in the formulation and presentation of a proposed solution for the central problem of this study. "Symbiosis" has been defined as:

> 2: mutual cooperation between persons and groups in a society especially when interdependence is involved.[1]

[1] Webster's third new international dictionary of the English language, unabridged (1966).

TABLE OF CONTENTS

CHAPTER I

INTRODUCTION

Nearly seven percent of the earth's land area is composed of islands that are situated in different manners and patterns. They can be arranged, geographically, in arcs, quadrangles, triangles and various linear and quasigeometric patterns.[1] Of interest is the fact that The Geographer of the United States Department of State has stated that "... each island group remains virtually unique ...."[2] Although islands and archipelagos will be defined and discussed in a later chapter, it is important to understand the dimension of total geographical area that these bodies encompass when related to other land areas such as continents. The islands of this planet number over 500,000 and have a combined geographical area in excess of 3,823,000 square miles and can vary in size from small surface areas to great land masses such as Greenland which is 840,000 square miles (i.e., larger in size than all but eleven countries of the world). There are 62 islands that have areas in excess of 4,000 square miles and at least 126 are larger in area than 1,000 square miles.[3]

Many of these islands fall into groups which are considered mid-ocean archipelagos and archipelagic States,[4] about which this study is concerned.

The traditional law of the sea terms used in customary and codified international law have been applied with greatest difficulty and with unsatisfactory results to mid-ocean archipelagos and independent archipelagic States in that these terms and rules were created to deal with continental masses, not with groups of mid-ocean islands. Whenever the archipelagic States desire to obtain the same access to mineral, fishery and other resources of the territorial and continental shelf areas as mainland-type countries enjoy, they find that it is impossible to apply the traditional terms and concepts in order to achieve justifiable results to themselves and to the international community as a whole. For example, Indonesia is approximately 3,275 miles in length, 1,375 miles in

[1] For a complete geographical discussion of islands and archipelagos, see: Islands: normal and special circumstances, The Geographer, Bureau of Intelligence and Research (INR), U.S. Department of State, RGES-3, December 10, 1973, Washington, D.C., 72 p.

[2] *Ibid.*, p. 6.

[3] *Ibid.*, p. 4.

[4] These terms are defined, respectively, in Chapter III and Chapter V.

width and consists of thousands of islands with no large continental land mass. The Indonesian government has declared that its islands and the waters lying between the islands consist of one unit,[5] with the waters between the islands treated as "internal" and the waters beyond the islands as "territorial."[6]

Such claims pose critical problems for the maritime nations, such as the United Kingdom, United States and U.S.S.R., who do not wish to have historic areas used for maritime commerce denied to navigational and other high-seas uses. An archipelagic State's action would be similar to an attempted blockade of areas of high seas and could provoke resistance, forcible measures and possible war.

Despite the gravity of the situation created by such claims and the uncertainty in the law, there is an incomplete and unsatisfactory analysis of the problem contained in the literature. In the few articles that do discuss the problem in depth, most of the authors approach the problem in terms of a bias in favor of treating an archipelagic State as one unit. They never consider mid-ocean archipelagos at all. Their articles are more of an attempt to defend the unilateral actions of Indonesia, the Philippines, Fiji and other archipelagic States whereby those countries proclaimed the jurisdictional competency to prescribe and enforce their laws over areas that were traditionally considered "high seas."[7]

In addition, there are a small number of specialized treatises that deal with law of the sea problems, exclusively:

Colombos, Constantine J., International law of the sea, 6th rev. ed. (1967);
Gidel, Gilbert C., Le droit international public de la mer (The public international law of the sea), vol. III, La mer territoriale et la zone contigue, 3 v. (1932);
Jessup, Philip C., The law of territorial waters and maritime jurisdiction (1927);
McDougal, M. and Wm. Burke, The public order of the oceans: a contemporary international law of the sea (1962);
Wenk, Edward, The politics of the ocean (1972).

However, these treatises contain a limited discussion (if any) of the problem presented here. Mainly, the authors engage in historical discussions with little analysis involved.

The general international law treatises usually contain a definition of an archipelago and a brief historical discussion.[8]

The casebooks and materials usually contain a short paragraph that refers to

[5] A complete discussion of the declaration is located in Chapter VI.

[6] A general discussion of traditional terms and governing concepts (e.g., internal waters, territorial sea, high seas, etc.) can be found in Chapter II.

[7] The term "high seas" is more fully examined in Chapter II.

[8] For example: Ian Brownlie, Principles of public international law, 2d ed. (1973); Charles C. Hyde, International law, 2d ed., vol. I (1945); D. P. O'Connell, International law, vol. I, 2d ed. (1970); L. F. L. Oppenheim, International law, a treatise, vol. I, Peace, 8th ed. (1952–1955); Georg Schwarzenberger, International law, 3rd ed. (1957–1968); and Marjorie Whiteman, Digest of international law, vol. 4 (1963).

the two judicial decisions dealing with archipelagos: *Anglo-Norwegian Fisheries* case, I.C.J. Reports 116 (1951); *CAB* v. *Island Airlines, Inc.* 235 F. Supp. 990 (D. Hawaii, 1964), affirmed 352 F.2d 735 (9th Cir., 1965).[9]

There are hundreds of articles dealing with the traditional terms and governing concepts discussed in this book (i.e., territorial waters, continental shelf, contiguous zones and high seas). A review of these articles reveals that the bulk of them do not touch upon the problem involved herein. A few articles do make a limited contribution:

Evensen, J., Certain legal aspects concerning the delimitation of the territorial waters of archipelagoes (1958);
Sorenson, M., The territorial sea of archipelagos (1959);
Coquia, J., The problem of the territorial waters of archipelagos (1959);
Syatauw, J., Some newly established Asian States and the development of international law (1961);
O'Connell, D. P., Mid-ocean archipelagos in international law (1973); and
Amerasinghe, C., The problem of archipelagoes in the international law of the sea (1974).

There is, of course, a vast amount of illustrative material and information in the public documents (both international and national). An exhaustive examination of these documents relevant to the problem of the law of the sea of territorial waters of archipelagos is made.

The methodology I employed in preparing this study is varied. In view of the history and difficult subject matter of the problem under examination, it is particularly necessary to examine vigorously the terminology and the influence of the terminology and definitions generally utilized. The subject matter does not lend itself to any particular methodology. Therefore, I will review and summarize the problem historically; analyze the competing interests involved; and based upon the foregoing, provide a critical analysis of a proposed solution.

It should also be noted that the problem requires that the rigorous analysis of the traditional legal terms and governing concepts employed and the influence of particular terms on the international community be conducted with the ultimate goal of accommodating the conflicting interests of the international community and the individual archipelagic States.[10]

The contribution which this study endeavors to make to the literature, therefore, is to identify the problem; to accommodate the conflicting and overlapping interests of the community; and, to propose a solution that is applicable to mid-ocean archipelagos and archipelagic States.

[9] The casebooks and materials include, for example, Wm. W. Bishop, Jr., International law cases and materials, 3rd ed. (1971); W. Friedman, O. Lissitzyn, R. Pugh, Cases and materials on international law (1969); Lester B. Orfield, Edward Re, Cases and materials on international law rev. ed. (1965); Ian Brownlie, Basic documents in international law, 2d ed. (1972); Herbert W. Briggs, The law of nations, cases, documents and notes, 2d ed. (1952).

[10] The effect of methodology on the structure of this book is set forth in Chapter V.

CHAPTER II

GENERAL DISCUSSION OF TRADITIONAL TERMS AND GOVERNING CONCEPTS REGARDING LAW OF THE SEA

Throughout this manuscript, certain law of the sea terms and governing concepts will be discussed and the proposals of the various authors and publicists analyzed. For the most part, the terms describe the jurisdictional authority of States. Although the terms are generally to be found in the law of the sea conventions, they are often used without definition. But as we have noted previously, the terms are not applicable to mid-ocean archipelagos or archipelagic States. The terms included in the conventions are incomplete and unsatisfactory. These terms are really words of art in the literature, with no complete agreement as to their meanings. In order to clarify the treatment, this chapter will be devoted to a brief discussion of the various terms as used in this study.

As may be seen on the attached chart appearing at page five, the jurisdictional competence to prescribe and enforce gradually becomes diminished as we move further seaward from the coast of a State (e.g., internal waters to territorial sea to high seas).

Internal waters are allocated totally to the coastal State (e.g., ports, harbors and roadsteads). The territorial sea is an area wherein the coastal State has full legal competence to prescribe and enforce its laws. The contiguous zone[1] is a gray area or zone located between the territorial sea and high seas. This zone is a special zone giving the coastal State competence to prescribe for special, limited purposes.[2] The zone is not more than twelve miles from the baseline. For example, if the territorial waters are three miles, the difference between twelve and three miles will equal nine miles—the size of the contiguous zone. If the territorial sea is six miles, the contiguous zone will be six miles. If the territorial sea is twelve miles, there will be no contiguous zone.

The geological continental shelf is a submarine continuation of the land mass. The seaward edge of the shelf and the start of the slope begin at an average water depth line of 200 meters (100 fathoms).[3] The shelf can also be

[1] Geneva Conference on Law of the Sea, 1958; Convention on the Territorial Sea and the Contiguous Zone.

[2] Fiscal, immigration, customs and sanitation. For a complete discussion of this zone, see *infra*, in this chapter.

[3] This depth line is a sufficiently characteristic basis for determining the area of the continental shelf. See John B. H. Wiseman and Cameron D. Ovey, Definitions of features on the deep-sea floor, 1 Deep-Sea Research 14 (1953).

discussed in terms of a ring around all continents, this said ring ranging from zero to more than 800 miles. Its average width is 30 miles and its total area is approximately 11 million square miles.[4] The shelves are not distributed evenly around each continent. Africa has the least expanse, whereas the eastern margins of North and South America have wide shelves. The western coasts of North and South America have practically no shelf area. The eastern coasts of the Asian and Australian continents have vast areas of continental shelf.[5]

Areas consisting of enclosed seas will not be discussed in this book because they do not have any connection with the development of the archipelagic problem. Therefore, the examination of these terms and concepts will commence with a discussion of internal waters.

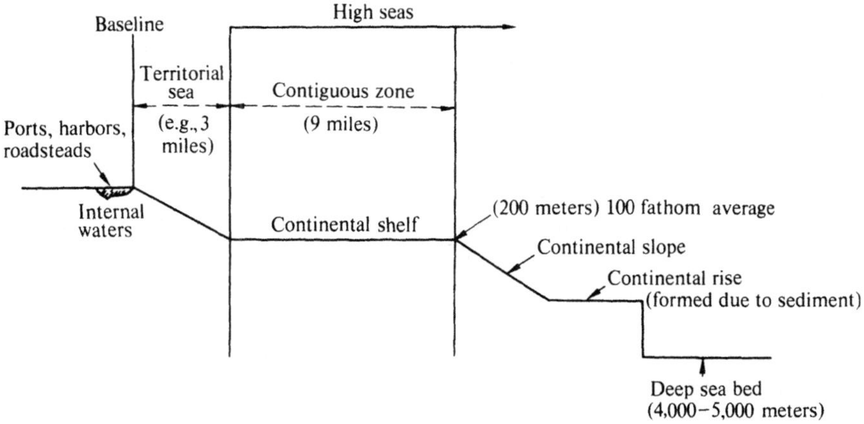

A diagram of diminishing jurisdictional authority from internal waters seaward

INTERNAL WATERS

The principal legal definition of internal waters is a description contained in Article 5(1), Convention on the Territorial Sea and the Contiguous Zone:[6]

Waters on the landward side of the baseline of the territorial sea form part of the internal waters of the State. (Article 5(1).)

Based upon conventional law, the two essential elements of internal waters are that (a) they be located immediately adjacent to the land territory of a State and

[4] Wallace E. Pratt, Petroleum on continental shelves, 31 Bull. Amer. Assn. Petroleum Geologists 658 (1947).

[5] This limited introductory discussion of the geological continental shelf is part of a broader analysis contained in: Z. J. Slouka, International custom and the continental shelf: a study in the dynamics of customary rules of international law (Martinus Nijhoff, The Hague, 1968) 186 p.

[6] This convention was adopted by the U.N. Conference on the Law of the Sea, April 29, 1958 (516 U.N. treaty series 205, Treaty No. I: 7477); 45 States have ratified as of October 28, 1974.

(b) because of their proximity to the State, the State exercises competence to prescribe and enforce its laws in a manner that is practically identical to its national jurisdictional competence.

The application of the two elements, for purposes of this study, can be observed by discussing the "claims" made by States in order to have the right to control access to their internal waters as well as to apply their authority to vessels in ports.[7]

Firstly, the main reason that States claim the right to control access to their internal waters is that these internal waters provide accessibility to a State's land territory. Therefore, the concern is for self-defense and security against infringement or encroachment. In connection therewith, and for the purpose of providing a basic awareness of the divergent opinions, there are at least three viewpoints regarding the claim to control access: namely, (a) to allow open access;[8] (b) to handle right of entry into ports, also implying rights to load and unload cargo and to embark and discharge passengers, as well;[9] and (c), State practice in recent centuries affords no indication that States may demand access to the ports of other States as a matter of right.[10]

Judicial precedent on the subject is practically nonexistent. There is one arbitration case[11] which held that every State must open ports to foreign merchant vessels, except in time of war.[12]

Thus far, the "access" discussion has been limited to a coastal State's jurisdictional competence but the problem of access to internal waters (i.e., ports, harbors and roadsteads) also involves landlocked States. In this regard, Article 3, Convention on the High Seas provides:

> In order to enjoy the freedom of the seas on equal terms with coastal States, States having no sea-coast should have free access to the sea. To this end States situated between the sea and a State having no sea-coast shall by common agreement with the latter and in conformity with existing international conventions accord:
> (a) To the State having no sea-coast, on a basis of reciprocity, free transit through their territory; and . . .[13]

[7] A more extensive discussion of State claims is contained in McDougal and Burke, Public order of the oceans: a contemporary international law of the sea, pp. 29, 30, 93, 94, 99–117.

[8] Grotius, The freedom of the seas 8, Magoffin transl. (1916).

[9] Colombos, International law of the sea 160, 5th rev. ed. (1962), 6th rev. ed. (1967), pp. 176–177.

[10] McDougal and Burke, *op. cit.*

[11] Arbitration between Saudi Arabia and the Arabian American Oil Company, Aramco (1958), 27 International law reports 117.

[12] Nevertheless, for the express purpose of resolving the problem involved here, it is necessary to maintain a basic understanding of the viewpoints presented because the concept of internal waters and jurisdictional competence to prescribe and enforce national law over internal waters is a "special interest" discussed in Chapter VII.

[13] Adopted by the U.N. Conference on Law of the Sea, April 29, 1958 (450 U.N. treaty series 82, Treaty No. I: 6465); 55 States have ratified as of October 28, 1974.

It is apparent that landlocked States have no coasts but do require access to ports.[14] Under Article 3, coastal States should attempt to agree upon access to ports with landlocked States. Since this right is perfected by "common agreement" under conventional law, the provision may be of limited benefit.

In summarizing "access" claims, it is necessary to point out that the viewpoint that is adhered to by a coastal State (or as a "special interest" of an archipelagic State or mid-ocean archipelago) regarding access should be considered in the light of States' desires to promote international commerce and navigation as much as possible. To deny access would mean an end to international maritime trade.

Assuming that a vessel is approaching or is located in a port, the next logical step for discussion involves a coastal State's right to apply its authority to approaching vessels or to vessels already located therein. When discussing this jurisdictional authority, it is essential to first categorize vessels as warships, merchant ships, private or governmental.

Warships are treated as a special category or class because they embody the symbolic sovereignty of a State.[15] Nevertheless, the sovereign coastal State can impose reasonable entry requirements prior to entry into port (e.g., length of permitted time in port, etc.).

Government ships other than warships are treated in the same manner as warships. Under customary international law, government ships (whether owned or operated) have no greater access to internal waters than warships.[16]

Once foreign vessels are located geographically within the port or harbor, the conditions listed for boarding a vessel in a port or harbor (i.e., internal waters) are similar to those conditions of boarding permitted to a coastal State under Article 19[17] (i.e., rules applicable to merchant ships) concerning a foreign ship passing through the territorial sea:[18]

1. The criminal jurisdiction of the coastal State should not be exercised on board a foreign ship passing through the territorial sea to arrest any person or to conduct any investigation in connexion with any crime committed on board the ship during its passage, save only in the following cases:

(a) If the consequences of the crime extend to the coastal State; or
(b) If the crime is of a kind to disturb the peace of the country or the good order of the territorial sea; or

[14] The special position of the landlocked States seens to have conferred more access to ports, harbors and roadsteads than that of maritime nations.

[15] A full discussion of the claims regarding control and the limitations thereon were discussed in *The Schooner Exchange* v. *McFaddon*, 11 U.S. (7 Cranch) 116 (1812).

[16] Private merchant vessels appear to be covered by the decision in the Aramco Arbitration (cited, *supra*, footnote 11). A broad discussion of access pursuant to vessel classification can be found in McDougal and Burke, *op. cit.*

[17] Convention on the Territorial Sea and the Contiguous Zone (cited, *supra*, footnote 6).

[18] Innocent passage is more fully discussed in this chapter, *infra*.

(c) If the assistance of the local authorities has been requested by the captain of the ship or by the consul of the country whose flag the ship flies; or
(d) If it is necessary for the suppression of illicit traffic in narcotic drugs.

(Article 19.)

Inasmuch as States have the highest degree of jurisdictional competence over internal waters, it is not surprising that States today have been claiming territorial sea areas and beyond as internal waters. As will be developed more fully, these claims are unilaterally pronounced in order to broaden a States' jurisdictional authority to encompass traditional high-seas areas containing mineral, fishing and other resources.

The next step on the diminishing scale of jurisdictional authority (from internal waters to high seas) of a coastal State must be approached by discussing the concept of a territorial sea.

TERRITORIAL SEA

The legal definition of territorial sea is stated in Articles 1 and 2, Convention on the Territorial Sea and Contiguous Zone:[19]

PART I. TERRITORIAL SEA

SECTION I. GENERAL

Article 1

1. The sovereignty of a State extends, beyond its land territory and its internal waters, to a belt of sea adjacent to its coast, described as the territorial sea. 2. This sovereignty is exercised subject to the provisions of these articles and to other rules of international law.

Article 2

The sovereignty of a coastal State extends to the air space over the territorial sea as well as to its bed and subsoil.

There are two problems concerning Articles 1 and 2 definition; namely, (a) there is no definite distance agreed upon (i.e., some States claim 200 miles, other States claim three miles, etc.); and (b), the wording of Article 1 ("The sovereignty of a State extends . . .") practically allows a coastal State complete competence to prescribe and enforce its rules over the breadth of the territorial sea.

The implications of the failure of States to agree upon a distance and uniformity regarding jurisdictional authority will be discussed later. Suffice it to say at this juncture that each time a State is desirous of expanding its jurisdictional authority seaward, it asserts a unilateral declaration that invariably increases the breadth of its territorial sea from three miles, for example, to 50 or 100 or

[19] Cited, *supra*, footnote 6.

200 miles. The declaration is made in order to gain exclusive access to mineral, fishery and other resources available in areas of high seas. Ultimately, this lack of uniformity could conceivably cause the termination of all law of the sea doctrines in international law.

Under conventional law, inland waters and territorial sea are divided from each other by use of baselines. Since the breadth of the territorial sea is measured from baselines, it is essential to understand (a) the two types of baselines employed under conventional law, (b) when each type is employed and (c) the permissible length of baselines, if any. As will be observed later, the major stumbling block in arriving at a satisfactory solution to the problem being presented at this time has been the lack of creativeness and the rigid employment of traditional terms and governing concepts to geographical areas that were never intended to be covered by conventional law.

BASELINES

Conventional law permits the use of baselines and sets forth two types of baselines (i.e., "normal" and "straight baselines") together with applicable conditions for use. Each kind of baseline accomplishes the same result, namely, the division of the territorial sea from inland waters.

The normal or traditional baseline for measuring the breadth of the territorial sea is the low-water line that runs along the coast of a State. In this connection, Article 3, Convention on the Territorial Sea and the Contiguous Zone[20] provides:

SECTION II. LIMITS OF THE TERRITORIAL SEA

Article 3

Except where otherwise provided in these articles, the normal baseline for measuring the breadth of the territorial sea is the low-water line along the coast as marked on large-scale charts officially recognized by the coastal State.

Illustrative of this type of baseline is the following example:

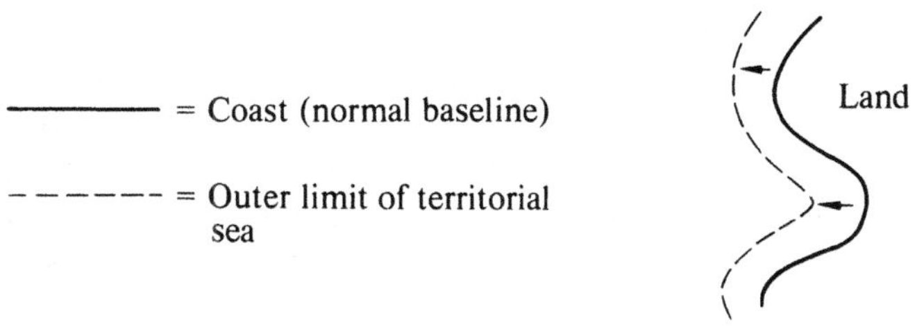

[20] *Ibid.*

It can be observed that the normal baseline coincides with the general configuration of the coast. The outer limit of the territorial sea, be it three or 200 miles, etc. is measured from the normal baseline. However, it is obvious that there are no islands or coastal archipelagos in the example given.

In 1951, the International Court of Justice rendered its opinion in the *Anglo-Norwegian Fisheries* case[21] and established the precedent for using the second type of baseline that is stated in conventional law; namely, the straight baseline:

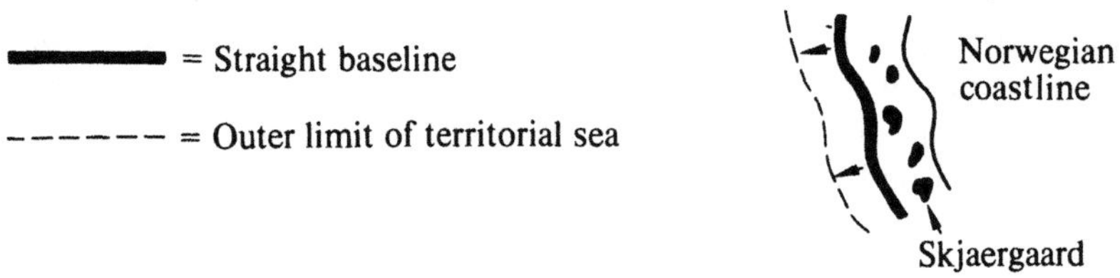

In the court's opinion, the term "skjaergaard", or the offshore fringe of islands, is a coastal archipelago located along the western sector of the Norwegian coast. For purposes of this study the facts of that case are that Norway relied heavily upon the waters off its coast for its fishing industry and precluded other nations from fishing within the area internal to the baselines as well as the area external to the baselines extending to the outer breadth of the territorial sea. The British argued, among other things, that the territorial sea should be measured from the normal low-water line and should not be measured seaward from the straight outer-island baselines employed by Norway. The court held that the Norwegians could, in fact, employ a system of straight baselines. The court, in effect, issued guidelines to States with similar geographical coasts. Straight baselines can be employed in localities where the coastline is deeply indented and cut into, or if there is a fringe of islands along the coast in its immediate vicinity if the following four criteria can be met: (a) close dependence on land domain; (b) straight baseline never departing from the general direction of the coast; (c) area so closely linked to the land domain as to be part of the internal waters; and (d) economic dependency on the land domain.

In 1958, only seven years after the *Anglo-Norwegian Fisheries* case, the Law of the Sea Conference was held in Geneva. Article 4, Convention on Territorial Sea and the Contiguous Zone,[22] in effect, codified the above-stated four criteria of the *Anglo-Norwegian Fisheries* case, with the result that the coastal archipelago (fringe of islands)/straight baseline formula is fully recognized under international law and is more generally applied throughout the world. Firstly, straight baselines are permissive, not mandatory. Under Article 4(1), it is

[21] I.C.J. reports 116 (1951).
[22] Cited, *supra*, footnote 6.

provided that they may be employed but are subject to the general standard of reasonableness:

1. In localities where the coastline is deeply indented and cut into, or if there is a fringe of islands along the coast in its immediate vicinity, the method of straight baselines joining appropriate points may be employed in drawing the baseline from which the breadth of the territorial sea is measured.

2. The drawing of such baselines must not depart to any appreciable extent from the general direction of the coast, and the sea areas lying within the lines must be sufficiently closely linked to the land domain to be subject to the regime of internal waters.

3. Baselines shall not be drawn to and from low-tide elevations, unless lighthouses or similar installations which are permanently above sea level have been built on them.

4. Where the method of straight baselines is applicable under the provisions of paragraph 1, account may be taken, in determining particular baselines, of economic interests peculiar to the region concerned, the reality and the importance of which are clearly evidenced by a long usage.

5. The system of straight baselines may not be applied by a State in such manner as to cut off from the high seas the territorial sea of another State. (Article 4.)[23]

. . .

The *Anglo-Norwegian Fisheries* case is of limited usefulness to this problem because the holding is limited to coastal archipelagos and fringe islands. As will be developed more fully later, rationale contained therein is erroneously analogized from coastal archipelagos to mid-ocean archipelagos and archipelagic States.

The Geographer of the United States Department of State, Bureau of Intelligence and Research, in his research study, Islands: normal and special circumstances,[24] reports that at least 60 coastal States employ straight baselines but that there is no uniform practice;[25] that Burma has a line segment measuring over 222 miles in length; and that, as of 1973, nearly 50 percent of the 34 States employing straight baseline systems employed one or more lines in excess of the 40-nautical-mile limit[26] stated in the *Anglo-Norwegian Fisheries* case:

	Nautical Miles		*Nautical Miles*
Dominican Republic	45.0	Thailand	59.15
Faeroes	60.8	Philippines	140.05
Burma	222.3	Iceland	74.0
Madagascar	123.0	Indonesia	124.0
Venezuela	98.9	Guinea	120.0
United Kingdom	40.25	Mauritania	89.0
Mozambique	60.4	Ecuador	136.0
Portuguese Guinea	79.0	Haiti	89.0

[23] It is observed that the fourth criterion, namely, economic dependency on the land domain, can only be taken into account under conventional law *after* the straight baseline method is found to be applicable.

[24] RGES-3, December 10, 1973, Washington, D.C., 72 p.

[25] Discussed, *supra*, in this chapter.

[26] Discussed, *infra*, in this chapter.

The right of innocent passage, however, is not affected by delimiting the baseline to the outside of the islands even though the establishment of straight baseline systems encloses areas that thereby become internal waters. Specifically, Article 5, Convention on the Territorial Sea and the Contiguous Zone[27] provides:

1. Waters on the landward side of the baseline of the territorial sea form part of the internal waters of the State.
2. Where the establishment of a straight baseline in accordance with article 4 has the effect of enclosing as internal waters areas which previously had been considered as part of the territorial sea or of the high seas, a right of innocent passage, as provided in articles 14 to 23 shall exist in those waters.

Despite the fact that the coastal State exercises practically complete control over its territorial sea, customary international law, in response to the needs of international navigation, has fully established the right to innocent passage.

INNOCENT PASSAGE

The conventional definition of innocent passage is given in Articles 14–15 of the Convention on the Territorial Sea and the Contiguous Zone:[28]

SECTION III. RIGHT OF INNOCENT PASSAGE

Sub-section A. Rules applicable to all ships

Article 14

1. Subject to the provisions of these articles, ships of all States, whether coastal or not, shall enjoy the right of innocent passage through the territorial sea.
2. Passage means navigation through the territorial sea for the purpose either of traversing that sea without entering internal waters or of proceeding to internal waters or of making for the high seas from internal waters.

. . .

4. Passage is innocent so long as it is not prejudicial to the peace, good order or security of the coastal State. Such passage shall take place in conformity with these articles and with other rules of international law.

. . .

Article 15

1. The coastal State must not hamper innocent passage through the territorial sea.

. . .

In order to determine innocence, Article 14 (4) looks to the "purpose" of the passage rather than to the act, itself. The definition is vague as to "innocence" because it is impossible to adopt a rule to apply equally in every situation. The

[27] Cited, *supra*, footnote 6.
[28] *Ibid.*

right of international navigation on the high seas would not have any practical meaning without the right of innocent passage through territorial waters, from the ports of one State to the ports of another State. However, according to conventional law, the determination of "innocence" is made, in the first instance, by the coastal State. The "passage" must not be prejudicial to the peace, good order or security of the coastal State.[29] State practice and community expectations are criteria applied by the flag and coastal States in order to assure continuity in international relations.

None of these rules is applicable to the innocent passage of foreign ships through international straits:

4. There shall be no suspension of the innocent passage of foreign ships through straits which are used for international navigation between one part of the high seas and another part of the high seas or the territorial sea of a foreign State.

There can be no suspension of this right under Article 16(4); whereas, the right can be suspended temporarily under Article 16(3) if international straits are not involved:

3. Subject to the provisions of paragraph 4, the coastal State may, without discrimination amongst foreign ships, suspend temporarily in specified areas of its territorial sea the innocent passage of foreign ships if such suspension is essential for the protection of its security. Such suspension shall take effect only after having been duly published.

This right of innocent passage becomes crucially important when examining the archipelagic States' proposals (Chapter V, *infra*), unilateral declarations (Chapter VI, *infra*), and when resolving the problem presented herein (Chapter VII, *infra*).

CONTIGUOUS ZONE

As was alluded to earlier in this chapter, a contiguous zone was created at the 1958 Law of the Sea Conference held in Geneva. This zone falls within the high seas that are adjacent to the coastal State and the conventional law gives the coastal State limited regulatory powers within the zone.

The definition of this zone is given in Article 24, Convention on the Territorial Sea and the Contiguous Zone:[30]

1. In a zone of the high seas contiguous to its territorial sea, the coastal State may exercise the control necessary to:
(a) Prevent infringement of its customs, fiscal, immigration or sanitary regulations within its territory or territorial sea;
(b) Punish infringement of the above regulations committed within its territory or territorial sea.

(Part II, Contiguous Zone, Article 24.)

[29] *Ibid.*, Article 14(4).
[30] Cited, *supra*, footnote 6.

Pursuant to the State practice which this article recognizes, the States have enumerated the four general functional areas of regulation and control in such a zone; namely, customs, fiscal, immigration and sanitation. An examination of the *travaux préparatoires* (legislative record) of the article, when taken with the clear application of the *inclusio unius exclusio alterius* rule in this instance, sharply limits the rights of States to these four functional areas in attempting to carve out such special jurisdictions in the high seas.

In addition, there is a twelve mile limit for the zone:

. . .

2. The contiguous zone may not extend beyond twelve miles from the baseline from which the breadth of the territorial sea is measured. (Article 24.)

This may be another reason to make it unnecessary to analyze the four functional limitations. As will be seen, they do not contribute to the development of the proposals or solutions that have been made with reference to the problem of the mid-ocean archipelago and archipelagic State. In any case, the concept of contiguous zone has been overtaken by the development of the economic zone or patrimonial sea and there is a probability that this concept will be substituted for the contiguous zone at the next law of the sea conference.

CONTINENTAL SHELF

At this point, reference should be made back to the schematic diagram appearing on page 5. Thus far, all discussion has been centered on the jurisdictional aspects of waters that are adjacent to a coastal State as sketched on that diagram. However, in certain areas of the world, valuable minerals and sedentary species of organisms are located not in the marine (water) areas but on or in the seabed and subsoil that is also adjacent to the coastal State. This area is known as the continental shelf.

The legal definition of continental shelf is given in Article 1, Convention on the Continental Shelf:[31]

For the purpose of these articles, the term 'continental shelf' is used as referring (a) to the seabed and subsoil of the submarine areas adjacent to the coast but outside the area of the territorial sea, to a depth of 200 metres or, beyond that limit, to where the depth of the superjacent waters admits of the said areas; (b) to the seabed and subsoil of similar submarine areas adjacent to the coasts of islands. (Article 1.)

There are tests in Article 1 that are used to determine if a coastal State may exploit the resources on a continental shelf. The seabed and subsoil of the shelf must be adjacent to the coast but outside the area of the territorial sea; the coastal State may exploit the resources on the shelf out to a depth of 200 meters; or, if the shelf is beyond 200 meters, the coastal State may exploit the

[31] 499 U.N. treaty series 311, Treaty No. I: 7302; 53 States have ratified as of October 28, 1974.

resources on the shelf out to a point where the shelf admits of exploitation. A State must meet these tests in order to exploit the legal continental shelf which may, or may not, meet the physical geography of the shelf.

The main problem with this definition occurs when attempting to define exploitability. How far out may a State exploit? In this regard, how does the 200 meter line move out?

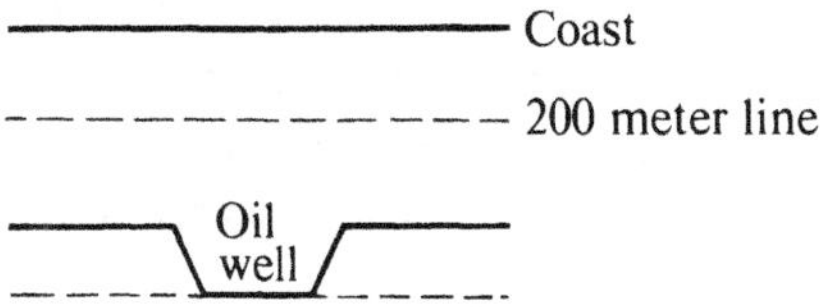

Looking at the above illustration, if oil is discovered, does the shelf move out as a whole or just where the well is located? Does exploitation mean an economic operating well rather than just test wells? If the line moves out on the eastern shoulder of the test well, does it do so on the western shoulder, as well? Does it affect other States' boundaries? How expansive and far reaching is an exploitation and its subsequent installations?[32] None of these questions has been answered. Therefore, the main problem regarding any discussion of the shelf comes when attempting to define the concept of "exploitability" and the area connotation.

There are certain statements that can be made concerning non-exploitive uses and jurisdictional authority over the shelf.

Article 2(4), Convention on Continental Shelf does not cover non-exploitive uses (e.g., underwater habitat):

4. The natural resources referred to in these articles consist of the mineral and other non-living resources of the seabed and subsoil together with living organisms belonging to sedentary species, that is to say, organisms which, at the harvestable stage, either are immobile on or under the seabed or are unable to move except in constant physical contact with the seabed or the subsoil.

[32] In his book International custom and the continental shelf, pp. 99–121, Mr. Slouka poses certain problems concerning, *inter alia*, exploitability; proof of exploitability; and exploitability and exploration: "... if the shelf resources, in a single area and a single instance, are successfully exploited under, for instance, 5,000 feet of water, does that depth determine the seaward limit of exclusive rights of all coastal states? ... [pp. 101–102]; If exploitation of coral reefs were undertaken at the maximum depth of 1,200 meters and then abandoned, after some meager results, for any reason: would then the depth of 1,200 meters be still considered the limit of exploitability until surpassed? ... [p. 104]; If a treaty member establishes the maximum limit of the shelf by proven exploitation at the depth of 1,500 feet, it obviously has no exclusive rights of exploration beyond that limit at a greater depth, but only inclusive rights together with any other use of the high seas. A foreign state or company may explore the deeper neighboring areas at will—but no more than that. It cannot exploit them because, under the wider meaning of the criterion of exploitability, it would automatically lose its inclusive rights of exploration and the coastal state's exclusive rights of exploration and exploitation would come into force [pp. 105–106].

The continental shelf rights are exclusive and accrue to the coastal State regardless of use or exploitation. In addition, the coastal State has control over minerals in the seabed plus control over sedentary species.[33]

The contiguous zone is located above and the continental shelf is located beneath waters known as high seas. The legal regime of the high seas is extremely significant in the development of the problem being presented. It is the cornerstone of law of the sea terminology. That is why when States decide to expand their territorial waters seaward or close off areas that were traditionally regarded as high seas, the interests of maritime nations in international navigation are affected immediately. For the purpose of setting forth law of the sea terms and governing concepts in this chapter, a brief discussion of this legal regime is necessary.

HIGH SEAS

The legal definition of high seas is given in Article 1, Convention on the High Seas[34] and provides:

> The term "high seas" means all parts of the sea that are not included in the territorial sea or in the internal waters of a State.

The basic freedom of the high seas doctrine was developed by Hugo Grotius[35] during the early part of the 17th century. His objective was to keep open trade and commerce routes for the Dutch. He argued that by natural law, the seas and resources contained therein belong to no individual State and should therefore be available for use by every State because of the vastness of the oceans. In other words, since no State can control all of the ocean space, there should be free access to it. Of course, Grotius' doctrine was based upon the conditions as they existed at that time.

Today, the high seas doctrine is being placed under increasing pressure with the discovery of minerals and sedentary species of organisms that are located not in the marine (water) areas but on or in the seabed and subsoil located beneath the high seas. The problem, basically, is: how do the States reach accommodations regarding these new uses? The conceptual approach to this problem in the convention is found in the use of the word "freedoms."

Article 2, Convention on the High Seas, is not restricted to the four freedoms listed therein. The freedoms are not absolute and must be exercised reasonably:

[33] "1. The coastal State exercises over the continental shelf sovereign rights for the purpose of exploring it and exploiting its natural resources.

2. The rights referred to in paragraph 1 of this article are exclusive in the sense that if the coastal State does not explore the continental shelf or exploit its natural resources, no one may undertake these activities, or make a claim to the continental shelf, without the express consent of the coastal State.

3. The rights of the coastal State over the continental shelf do not depend on occupation, effective or notional, or on any express proclamation. (Article 2, cited, *supra*, footnote 31.)

[34] Cited, *supra*, footnote 13.

[35] *Op. cit.*

> The high seas being open to all nations, no State may validly purport to subject any part of them to its sovereignty. Freedom of the high seas is exercised under the conditions laid down by these articles and by the other rules of international law. It comprises, inter alia, both for coastal and non-coastal States:
>
> (1) Freedom of navigation;
> (2) Freedom of fishing;
> (3) Freedom to lay submarine cables and pipelines;
> (4) Freedom to fly over the high seas.
>
> These freedoms, and others which are recognized by the general principles of international law, shall be exercised by all States with reasonable regard to the interests of other States in their exercise of the freedom of the high seas. (Article 2.)

Other examples of freedoms include scientific research, farming of the sea, mining, man's habitat, petroleum products, disposal of wastes, movement of freight, weapons testings and intelligence reports concerning weapons.

Restrictions on the freedoms are established by either multilateral agreement (e.g., international rules of the road; slave transport; piracy and ocean dumping) or unilaterally.

The guidelines used in order to determine if unilateral restrictions are acceptable under international law are (a) reasonableness and (b) determination if the act does not violate the true purpose of the freedom of the seas doctrine. In order to determine the reasonableness of any State action, the question presented is what is the primary object of the action taken? In order to determine if the act does not violate the true purpose of the freedom of the seas doctrine, the question presented is: does the act, in fact, interfere with freedom of navigation, access to ocean resources or any other freedom listed in Article 2?

In later chapters, there will be extensive discussion of unilateral declarations and acts pertaining thereto by archipelagic States and the protests made by the maritime nations. These declarations and acts having occurred, the purpose of this study is to resolve the problem presented in a workable manner in order to assure that the threat to international order, posed by the problem, no longer exists.

CHAPTER III

GENERAL DISCUSSION OF THE LAW OF TERRITORIAL WATERS OF ISLANDS AND COASTAL ARCHIPELAGOS AS DISTINGUISHED FROM THE LAW OF TERRITORIAL WATERS OF MID-OCEAN ARCHIPELAGOS AND ARCHIPELAGIC STATES

The relevant law of the sea terms and governing concepts, as said terms and concepts are used throughout this manuscript, have been reviewed in the last chapter. Now, it is necessary to understand some of the law of the sea problems of islands and coastal archipelagos in order to comprehend the more complex laws of the sea regarding mid-ocean archipelagos and archipelagic States.

The traditional terms and governing concepts that are reviewed in this chapter regarding coastal archipelagos, fringe islands, etc. are more directly basic to the discussion of the thesis problem regarding mid-ocean archipelagos and archipelagic States. This is so because most of the preparatory materials submitted for use at the Hague and Geneva Conferences held in 1930 and 1958, respectively, did not distinguish between coastal and mid-ocean archipelagos. As will be discussed more fully in Chapter IV, most publicists, legal writers and government proposals (Chapter V) analogize the problem of territorial waters of mid-ocean archipelagos and archipelagic States with that of coastal archipelagos. As will be seen more fully later, this misleading argument by analogy was a result of historical circumstances, in particular, colonial circumstances, which will be noted later.[1]

This chapter is limited to the geographical considerations and is developed by using the same process as the preceding chapter, but these concepts and terms are more immediately important and therefore serve as a bridge to the main development of the problem.

Before entering into a discussion regarding the law of territorial waters of islands and coastal achipelagos, and the problems associated therewith, it is necessary to set forth conventional and other definitions regarding islands and archipelagos. As will be seen later in the discussion, one of the basic elements of an archipelago is that it be composed of islands. Therefore, the discussion commences with the basic definition of an "island."

[1] See Chapter IV.

DEFINITIONS

Of an Island

The legal definition of an island is stated in Article 10, Convention on the Territorial Sea and the Contiguous Zone.[2] This article defines an island as:

> ... a naturally formed area of land, surrounded by water, which is above water at high tide.

The Convention excludes such formations as spoil banks resulting from dredging operations and artificial islands. It is also apparent that an artificially constructed area cannot be considered as an island. In other words, to come within the meaning of the definition, the lands must be surrounded by water and must be above water at high tide. Although not otherwise specifically provided for, it is safe to assert that neither habitability, geographic shape, square mileage, nor soil texture of an island are considered by conventional law for the purposes of delimiting the territorial sea. Size and capacity for use have no relevance in the determination.[3]

On the other hand, The Geographer of the United States State Department,[4] after considering the fact that islands can be rather large in size and because The Geographer conceives islands as mainlands which have all the legal-geographic attributes of continents, categorizes islands and smaller formations by their size and defines all of these formations as follows:

1) *rocks*, less than ·001 square mile in area;
2) *islets*, between ·001 and 1 square mile;
3) *isles*, greater than 1 square mile but not more than 1,000 square miles; and
4) *islands*, larger than 1,000 square miles.[5]

Therefore, because of their large size, islands are defined and conceived by The Geographer as mainlands which have all of the legal-geographic attributes of continents. The Geographer is clearly linking the geographical description to the legal concepts since all four of the categories have territorial seas under conventional international law.

Setting aside the conventional law and The Geographer's viewpoint, islands have been defined in somewhat different manners. For the purpose of determining the ownership of new islands formed in a navigable stream, it has been held that land surrounded by water only in times of high water is not an island

[2] Adopted by the U.N. Conference on the Law of the Sea, April 29, 1958 (516 U.N. Treaty Series 205, Treaty No. I: 7477); 45 States have ratified as of October 28, 1974.

[3] A more complete analysis of the definition of an island is located in McDougal and Burke, Public order of the oceans, p. 314.

[4] Islands: normal and special circumstances, The Geographer, Bureau of Intelligence and Research (INR), U.S. Department of State, RGES–3, December 10, 1973, Washington, D.C., 72 p.

[5] *Ibid.*, p. 17.

within the rule that the State takes title to such lands;[6] for the purpose of mapping and charting, an island has been defined as,

> ... a body of land extending above and completely surrounded by water at the mean high-water stage; an area of dry land entirely surrounded by water or a swamp; an area of swamp entirely surrounded by open water.[7]

Other definitions are rather ludicrous but illustrate the problem involved:

> By an island should be understood a land surface, rocky or otherwise, covered or not covered with water, connected or unconnected with the continent, over which it is impossible to navigate.[8]

One author states that:

> Law cannot say what a bay is, or an archipelago, or a strait, or a mountain, or indeed a mole-hill. The business of law is to decide, given a bay, however the fact of the bay may be determined, what are the legal consequences of the bay.... To endeavor to clothe geographical definitions with scientific exactitude and to impute to them legal validity is the way of hindrance and not of aid to the progressive codification of international law. The codification of international law is a process and like other processes it must go forward by means of trial and error....[9]

Treatises use the conventional definition contained in Article 10, Convention on the Territorial Sea and the Contiguous Zone.[10]

Of an Archipelago

Whereas the legal definition of an island is contained in Article 10, Convention on the Territorial Sea and the Contiguous Zone, there has been no attempt to define an archipelago in conventional law.[11] However, a definition was prepared by a Norwegian lawyer, Jens Evensen,[12] in a preparatory document that was later submitted by the Secretariat of the United Nations at the 1958

[6] *Payne* v. *Hall*, Sup. Ct. Iowa. 12/13/21. No. 34233, 185 N.W. 912 (1921); *McBride* v. *Steinweden*, Sup. Ct. Kansas, 1/6/06, 83 P. 822 (1906). See discussion contained in Shalowitz's work, Shore and sea boundaries, vol. I, pp. 225–229.

[7] See Edmonston, Nautical chart manual 77, U.S. Coast and Geodetic Survey, 1956. These definitions are located in Shalowitz's publication, *op. cit.*

[8] League of Nations Document, C.74. M.39. 1929. V. vol. II, p. 53.

[9] Reeves, The codification of the law of territorial waters, 24 Am. J.I.L. 486 (1930), pp. 497–498.

[10] Cited, *supra*, in footnote 2.

[11] The reason for this result is due to the problems that confronted the States at the 1930 and 1958 Conferences. A full discussion of the historical and traditional approaches to the application of the law of territorial waters of mid-ocean archipelagos and archipelagic States occurs in the next chapter.

[12] The preparatory document was a study concerning archipelagos: Certain legal aspects concerning the delimitation of the territorial waters of archipelagos, U.N. Doc. A/CONF. 13/18, U.N. Conference on the Law of the Sea, Preparatory documents 1958, (1958), vol. I.

Law of the Sea Conference held in Geneva. In this document, an archipelago was defined as:

... a formation of two or more islands (islets or rocks), which geographically may be considered as a whole.[13]

This definition was not even discussed formally, let alone adopted, at the 1958 Conference. One of the main problems with this definition was that there was no justification presented that was acceptable to the participating States regarding the treatment of an archipelago "... as a whole."

On the other hand, The Geographer's approach, as indicated by The Geographer, United States Department of State, defines an archipelago as consisting of certain "characteristics":

—There must be a substantial number of relatively large islands scattered throughout a sea in an areal and not a linear pattern;
—The islands should be situated so as to relate geographically (adjacency) to each other and to others in the group; and
—They should be perceived as a unitary whole because of political administration.[14]

Notwithstanding the fact that The Geographer presents this definition, he realizes that it is "general" and could lead to "abuse."[15] In order to deal with these limiting factors, he states that archipelagos could conceivably be treated as "special circumstances":[16]

The most important characteristics of an archipelago would be:
—Areal dispersion of many islands over two or more axes (longitudinal and lateral);
—Adjacency of islands among themselves with special reference to the length of the line about the perimeter; and
—A land/water or territorial sea/insular sea ratio contained within the ultimate archipelagic baselines system.

Having observed that there is no conventional definition, although Jens Evensen's document was presented to the 1958 Law of the Sea Conference, and that The Geographer defines an archipelago in terms of "characteristics," it is necessary to set forth a sample of mainland-type States' practice regarding the treatment of their outlying islands (i.e., mid-ocean archipelagos).

The treatises usually adopt Jens Evensen's definition[17] or do not contain a definition.

Also, it must be recognized that whether or not a formation or grouping of islands is or is not an archipelago has been determined not by the formal process of definition but on the basis of history or by occupation and

[13] *Ibid.*, p. 5.
[14] See: Islands: normal and special circumstances, p. 27.
[15] *Ibid.*
[16] *Ibid.*, pp. 27–28. The Geographer's proposal will be discussed, in detail, in Chapter V.
[17] In: Certain legal aspects of the territorial waters of archipelagos.

use.[18] For example, the islands de los Canarios, on the south coast of Cuba, span from the Jardines Bank to Cape Frances and comprise an area of over one hundred miles, containing some islands, but mainly containing banks upon which the depth of the water is not able to permit navigation. These islands and banks are treated as an archipelago, by Cuba, and the territorial waters of Cuba run along the outer edge of these banks.[19]

Even in the situations where archipelagos do exist, the treatment afforded to them by their respective territorial governments may vary. For example, the Ecuadorean Government[20] set a twelve-mile breadth of territorial waters and established baselines around the Galapagos Islands (i.e., Colon Archipelago) so that the archipelago is treated as a single unit.

In the United States, the United States District Court of Hawaii held in *Civil Aeronautics Board* v. *Island Airlines*[21] that waters that are situated between the Hawaiian island chain, beyond the three-mile limit, are considered high seas and thereby rejected the contention that these channels of water constituted a territorial sea.

Therefore, these two examples of State practice suggest that there is no uniformity in mainland-type States' treatment of their mid-ocean archipelagic territory.

If the States are not acting in accord regarding this treatment, it follows that the specific problem of delimitation by baselines[22] (as to whether straight baselines can be employed) and the problems concerning rights to having a territorial sea or internal waters designated within any of the four geographic areas discussed in this chapter; namely, (1) an island adjacent to a coast; (2) artificial structures as islands; (3) islands, rocks, promontories that are part of a coastal configuration; and (4), offshore islands, will not result in a uniform State practice. An understanding of the existence of these problems will be useful when analyzing the delimitation problems of mid-ocean archipelagos and archipelagic States during subsequent chapters.[23]

AN ISLAND ADJACENT TO A COAST

Where an island is adjacent to a coast, some States treat the area between the island and the coast as internal waters. Thus, such an island becomes important to delimitation of water boundaries because that island is considered to be part

[18] See Colombos, International law of the sea 120, 121, 6th rev. ed. (1967).

[19] Cuba also treats the waters situated between the Cuban Cays (string of islands, islets and reefs) as internal.

[20] By virtue of a law enacted on February 21, 1951 (U.N. legislative series, Laws and regulations of the regime of the territorial sea (1957), p. 13).

[21] 235 F. Supp. 990 (D. Hawaii, 1964), affirmed 352 F. 2d 735 (9th Cir. 1965).

[22] See Chapter II.

[23] For the purpose of setting forth the diverging viewpoints of State practice in connection with the four geographic areas, it is useful to adopt an approach that is similar to the "claim-counterclaim" and delimitation of baselines discussions as more fully discussed in: McDougal and Burke, Public order of the oceans, pp. 305–445.

of the coastline so that the baseline for the territorial sea includes the island. Other States assert that the mere presence of an island adjacent to a coast does not merit the creation of an area of such high degree of jurisdictional competence. These States maintain that even if the baseline is extended to the island, the waters within the baselines are only part of the territorial sea and not of internal waters.

ARTIFICIAL STRUCTURES AS ISLANDS

Illustrative of State practice is the viewpoint espoused by States that are desirous of using artificial structures as if they were islands for delimitation purposes (e.g., where a formation is below water at high tide it may be used for baseline purposes if an artificial structure is built upon it; another example is of structures built on the ocean floor such as buildings erected upon pilings that are placed into the seabed). Other states assert that the coastal State would have too much discretion to extend its jurisdictional limits seaward.

There are special problems concerning the "island" concept regarding artificial islands and artificial or permanent structures. Turning first to artificial or man-made islands, the main problem is if the territorial sea may be measured from these man-made islands that are always above water, and if an area that is temporarily submerged may be allowed a belt of territorial sea.[24] In this situation, the question is if the artificially created area is constructed for practical use or if it is merely an attempt to extend the territorial sea or internal waters without considering the relationship to any local interest that may be involved. McDougal and Burke suggest[25] that the problem in considering if any credence for delimitation purposes ought to be given to formations and structures other than natural islands is if these formations and structures give the coastal State any competence to prescribe and enforce its rules in the surrounding waters that would not otherwise be viable under international law. Their conclusion is that land or rock formations that surface at a level that is not high tide would not be enough reason to establish any extra local interest, jurisdictionally, in adjacent waters. The mere fact that some off-shore, low tide elevations exist should not result in giving the coastal State any additional competence in the waters between the offshore, low-tide elevations and the shore, nor should their mere existence create any particular competence in the seaward waters. Therefore, these formations are not to be taken into account when measuring the breadth of the territorial waters or in determining the extent of internal waters.

[24] This problem is distinguishable from the facts in *United States* v. *Ray*, 423 F. 2d 16 (5th Cir. 1970), wherein the defendant was desirous of creating a new country on an island dredged from soil off of the southeast coast of Florida. There, the court granted an injunction that prohibited construction on reefs that were located beyond the three mile limit because, among other reasons, the defendants failed to obtain a permit from the Army Corps of Engineers as provided under the River and Harbors Act of 1899.

[25] McDougal and Burke, *op. cit.*, pp. 387–388.

Before discussing any conventional law regarding artificial or man-made islands, the subject of permanent structures arises within the geographic context of artificial structures as islands.

Permanent structures that are above water, built on low-tide elevations or upon the ocean floor (e.g., lighthouses and oil installations) normally do not require any extension of the territorial sea. Nevertheless, it has been asserted that oil installations and marker buoys (i.e., navigational aids) may require that the coastal State be given competence to prescribe and enforce its jurisdictional claims because of (a) navigational hazards and (b) possible interference by other States. This does not necessarily imply that the coastal State need extend the breadth of its territorial waters. Perhaps a jurisdictional boundary around the installations and buoys would suffice. Presently, however, there is nothing in conventional law authorizing this unilateral declaration of boundary delimitation.

Within the same area of special problems regarding artificial islands and artificial or permanent structures, a discussion of the current conventional law is appropriate in order to observe the treatment, if any, that these problems received at the 1958 Law of the Sea Conference held in Geneva.

Basically, the discussion is centered upon artificial islands and permanent structures, the types of formations that usually are surrounded by water and that could conceivably require larger areas from which the territorial sea would be measured. In this connection, Articles 4(3) and 11, Convention on the Territorial Sea and the Contiguous Zone[26] contain the current law on the subject:

> 3. Baselines shall not be drawn to and from low-tide elevations, unless lighthouses or similar installations which are permanently above sea level have been built on them. (Article 4.)

> 1. A low-tide elevation is a naturally formed area of land which is surrounded by and above water at low-tide but submerged at high tide. Where a low-tide elevation is situated wholly or partly at a distance not exceeding the breadth of the territorial sea from the mainland or an island, the low-water line on that elevation may be used as the baseline for measuring the breadth of the territorial sea.
>
> 2. Where a low-tide elevation is wholly situated at a distance exceeding the breadth of the territorial sea from the mainland or an island, it has no territorial sea of its own. (Article 11.)

Illustrative of Article 11(1) and (2) is the following example:

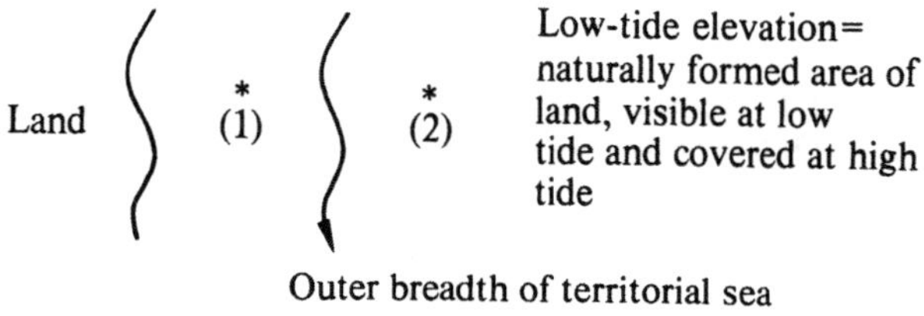

[26] Cited, *supra*, footnote 2.

If the low-tide elevation is located within the margin of the territorial sea (i.e. at (1)), the outer margin of the territorial sea can be measured seaward from the low-tide elevation thereby extending the breadth of the territorial sea from the original distance. Thus, the low-tide elevation is treated as a baseline in this example. However, if the low-tide elevation is located outside the breadth of the territorial sea (i.e. at (2)), the low-tide elevation cannot be used to extend the breadth of the territorial sea even though a State may exercise exclusive sovereignty over the area. In addition, there is no provision for a low-tide elevation to have its own territorial sea under conventional law.

Regarding islands,[27] Article 10(2) of the Convention on the Territorial Sea and the Contiguous Zone[28] provides:

2. The territorial sea of an island is measured in accordance with the provisions of these articles.

The purpose of Article 10(2) is to state that the territorial sea will be measured from an island without giving every island its own belt of jurisdictional competence.

Thus far, the discussion has centered upon the special problems concerning two of the four geographic areas; namely, an island adjacent to a coast and artificial structures as islands. Mainly, the two areas that were discussed were not part of a more complex coastal configuration that consisted of many geographic patterns. The special problems that occur in the last two geographic areas (i.e., islands, rocks, promontories that are part of a coastal configuration and offshore islands), are more complex because of their physical location and proportionate size.

ISLANDS, ROCKS, PROMONTORIES THAT ARE PART OF A COASTAL CONFIGURATION

The traditional problem concerning these geographic areas revolves around determining whether these configurations produce internal waters or territorial seas.[29]

Rugged and complex geographical configurations can be found in the northeastern United States and north-western United States, including Alaska, in Scandinavian areas such as Norway,[30] and elsewhere. Geographically, this type of coast is either (a) composed of frequent indentations that penetrate the entire coastal region, or (b) consists of many islands and rocks adjacent to a coast, or, (c) is a combination of (a) and (b). Some States assert the view that

[27] Article 10(1) of the Convention on the Territorial Sea and the Contiguous Zone is discussed *supra*, in this chapter.

[28] Cited, *supra*, footnote 2.

[29] McDougal and Burke, *op. cit.*, pp. 327–373, 398–411.

[30] For example, the "Skjaergaard" (coastal archipelago) consists of some 120,000 islands, rocks and islets and extends along most of the Norwegian coastline.

they may use a system of straight lines in order to connect various features of the configurations due to the States' dependence on the ocean. This view is generally based upon a close relationship between the mainland and adjacent sea areas which can be traced to geographical similarities such as climate, marine environment and resources.

As was alluded to earlier, conventional international law regarding islands, rocks and promontories is an outgrowth and codification of the *Anglo-Norwegian Fisheries* case.[31] The *Anglo-Norwegian Fisheries* case emphasized the complex character of the coasts of Norway. The decision also set forth the relationship of the waters to the social processes on adjacent land areas. In spite of the decision, State practice regarding the treatment of baselines in front of coasts deeply indented or fringed by islands[32] is varied.

Relying upon the *Anglo-Norwegian Fisheries* case at the 1958 Law of the Sea Conference, Article 4(1) of the Convention on the Territorial Sea and the Contiguous Zone was adopted. This Article states that:

> In localities where the coastline is deeply indented and cut into, or if there is a fringe of islands along the coast in its immediate vicinity, the method of straight baselines joining appropriate points may be employed in drawing the baseline from which the breadth of the territorial sea is measured.

In addition, Article 4(5) provides that a straight-line system cannot be drawn:

> in such a manner as to cut off from the high seas the territorial sea of another state.

As a practical matter, this prohibits States from seeking to extend their jurisdictional competences over the navigation of ships making for or leaving the ports of a neighboring State.

CONTROVERSIES ARISING OUT OF THE LEGAL TREATMENT OF GROUPS OF OFFSHORE ISLANDS

The last geographical area to be discussed, in order to present the special problems regarding the law of territorial waters of island and coastal archipelagos, involves groups of offshore islands.[33] In connection with groups of offshore islands (and despite the contents of Article 10(2), Convention on the Territorial Sea and the Contiguous Zone)[34] States insist that the group of offshore islands forms a unit and that the baseline for the territorial sea should be measured from point to point along the most distant outlying islands. Thus, all waters within the baseline would be considered internal waters. Contrary to

[31] See discussion contained in Chapter II.
[32] See list of baseline variations employed by different States in Chapter II.
[33] McDougal and Burke, *op. cit.*, pp. 373–387.
[34] Cited, *supra*, in footnote 2.

this view, other States maintain that each island, irrespective of its distance from any other island, should have its own territorial sea.[35]

Many of the special problems in areas of this geographic type arise from overlapping and non-overlapping territorial seas of groups of offshore islands. With regard to overlapping territorial seas, a large number of States claim that each island should have its own territorial sea. Thus, an island within the territorial sea that is measured from either another island or the mainland extends the territorial sea outward. Also, if the island is within a distance equal to twice the width of the territorial sea, then the claimed areas of territorial sea overlap. Overlapping occurs when the adjacent features are islands or when one is an island and the other a mainland coast. The problem arises where an island or group of islands is in some degree of proximity to each other or to the mainland. In this connection, there is some State practice which treats these overlapping island(s) as one unit with other relevant features for measuring the territorial sea. The waters to the mainland side are then considered internal waters. The territorial sea is measured outward from the seaward side of the islands. Where the distances separating offshore islands exceed the combined belts of the territorial sea, a few States contend that the territorial sea can be extended further in order to eliminate the strip of high seas between them.

There are occasions where, to the contrary, overlapping of groups of offshore islands does not occur, that is, where there are only a few adjacent islands whose areas of territorial sea do not overlap with each other but do join with the territorial sea of a mainland. Here, the problem, when considering the islands as one unit, is whether the coastal State should be allowed to incorporate these areas of the high seas within internal waters or within the territorial sea.

In summary, the special problems concerning the four geographic areas presented herein do not have definite answers thereto. They were set forth in order to introduce the subject matter of this study regarding the delimitation problems of mid-ocean archipelagos and archipelagic States. Having reviewed the traditional terms and governing concepts, as used throughout this book (i.e., Chapter II), and thereafter presenting definitions of islands and archipelagos, in general, together with the problems regarding the various geographic areas located near a coastal State (as distinguished from a mid-ocean archipelago and archipelagic State), in order to serve as a conduit or bridge between these problems and the main development of the problem presented herein, it is now necessary to commence upon a review of the historical and traditional approaches to the application of the law of territorial waters of mid-ocean archipelagos and archipelagic States.

[35] Names and attitudes of various States will be discussed in the next two chapters. It will be quite obvious that the "special interests" of the archipelagic States and the "general interests" of the maritime nations dictate viewpoints toward resolving these problems. Interestingly enough, these viewpoints are not necessarily uniform in nature.

CHAPTER IV

A REVIEW OF THE HISTORICAL AND TRADITIONAL APPROACHES TO THE APPLICATION OF THE LAW OF TERRITORIAL WATERS OF MID-OCEAN ARCHIPELAGOS AND ARCHIPELAGIC STATES

The traditional legal terms and governing concepts have been set forth as well as an introduction to the special problems regarding component parts of an archipelago. It is now necessary to present a complete review of the historical and traditional approaches to the application of the law of territorial waters to mid-ocean archipelagos and archipelagic States. The influence of the legal terms and governing concepts on the international community will become apparent as this chapter develops from a discussion commencing with the contributions, if any, of the various private scientific and scholarly organizations and terminating with a review of the viewpoints of publicists and legal writers. Every effort has been made to present all of the materials regarding archipelagos in this chapter. The review of all of the materials and contributions will make it apparent that (a) in most instances, the sources have not and do not distinguish between coastal and mid-ocean archipelagos and (b), there is a degree of rigidity (or adherence to the traditional terms but not necessarily to the governing concepts) that prevents any practical and workable solution to the problem being presented at this time. Nevertheless, each of the discussions in the private scholarly and scientific organizations, and, in particular, the draft articles produced at each of the conferences, is important and relevant to the proposal being made in this study because each article demonstrates a problem that was raised at a particular international conference or at committee level. As will be seen, some of the problems are repetitious, having lingered at international conferences without being resolved, and none of these problems was resolved in a satisfactory manner to either the special interest (i.e. archipelagic States) or general interest groups (i.e. maritime nations).

The first recorded recognition of the problem of the law of territorial waters of archipelagos took place at the private meetings of various scientific and scholarly organizations.

PRIVATE SCIENTIFIC AND SCHOLARLY ORGANIZATIONS

L'Institut de Droit International

The Fifth Committee of the Institute met at the Lausanne Conference during 1927 (with Sir Thomas Barclay and Professor Alejandro Alvarez serving as Rapporteurs). The Committee proposed Article 5 of the *Travaux Preparatoires*[1] *(premiere partie), concernant un projet de reglement relatif a la mer territoriale*:

Where a group of islands belong to one coastal State and where the islands of the periphery of the group are not further apart from each other than the double breadth of the marginal sea, this group shall be considered a whole and the extent of the marginal sea shall be measured from a line drawn between the uttermost parts of the islands.[2]

This draft article is rather negative in scope in that (a) the "group of islands" belonging to a coastal State is actually a coastal archipelago; (b) the islands must not be further than six miles from each other (i.e. double the breadth of marginal sea as it was generally accepted at that time);[3] (c) the article does not discuss any maximum distance from the coastal State and, of course, (d) the islands cannot be too distant from each other or they will not be considered as a "group".

An amendment to Article 5 of the *Travaux Preparatoires (deuxieme partie concernant un projet de reglement relatif a la mer territorial* was tendered at the Stockholm Conference of 1928 and the subject of the amendment concerned coastal archipelagos:

In case an archipelago is situated along the coast of a country the extent of the marginal seas shall be measured from the outermost islands and rocks, provided that the distance of the islands and islets situated nearest to the coast does not exceed the double breadth of the marginal seas.[4]

The amendment did not state a maximum distance between the islands of an archipelago, but it did suggest a distance of twice the breadth of the territorial seas between the nearest island of the archipelago and the mainland.

The basic flaw in this article, however, is that the outer fringe of the islands could conceivably extend hundreds of miles from the coastal State. The

[1] The conference used the term *Travaux Preparatoires* not in the usual sense but as a title for the various specific drafts and projects discussed at the conference.

[2] Annuaire de L'Institut, vol. 33, part 1, 1927, p. 81. The translation from the French is that of Jens Evensen as published in his: Certain legal aspects concerning the delimitation of the territorial waters of archipelagoes, U.N. Doc. A/CONF. 13/18, U.N. Conf. on the Law of the Sea, Preparatory docs. 1958 (1958), vol. I, p. 7.

[3] The term "territorial sea" has replaced the term "marginal sea" and will be used in this book even when discussing a draft or formulation utilizing the term "marginal sea."

[4] Annuaire de L'Institut, vol. 34 (1928), p. 647; as translated by Mr. Evensen, *op. cit.*, p.

draftsmen apparently had in mind that the article would apply only to coastal archipelagos, that is to say, to archipelagos located along the mainland coast of the State.

The final resolution at the Institute contained Article 5, paragraph 2, which is a combination of the first article presented and its amendment and the resolution appears to be applicable to a few geographical patterns only:

> Where archipelagos are concerned, the extent of the marginal sea shall be measured from the outermost islands or islets provided that the archipelago is composed of islands and islets not further apart from each other than twice the breadth of the marginal sea and also provided that the islands and islets nearest to the coast of the mainland are not situated further out than twice the breadth of the marginal sea.[5]

A majority of the Institute at the meeting held in Stockholm during 1928 considered the territorial sea to be three nautical miles rather than six nautical miles. Thus, the grouping of islands falling within Article 5(2) would be rather closely spaced. The significance of baseline lengths will be noted later.

International Law Association

The Executive Council of the International Law Association appointed a Neutrality Committee on January 8, 1924 with Professor Alejandro Alvarez serving as chairman. The assignment of the committee was to consider the question of "Territorial waters and maritime jurisdiction" and to present Draft Regulations.

At the 1924 meeting of the International Law Association held in Stockholm, the committee reported under the title: The laws of maritime jurisdiction in time of peace. The Committee's draft convention contained no definitive provisions with respect to territorial waters of archipelagos.[6] The draft provided in Article 2 only that:

> States shall exercise jurisdiction over their territorial waters to the extent of three marine miles from low water mark at spring tide along their coasts.

However, the draft also provided in Article 3, concerning islands located outside

> the territorial limit of a State, [that] a zone of territorial waters shall be measured round each of the said islands.

A special draft convention, however, was submitted separately by Professor Alvarez which differed from the committee's proposal.[7]

[5] Annuaire de L'Institut, vol. 34, p. 673; the translation is again that of Mr. Evensen, *op, cit.*, p. 8.

[6] Report of 33rd Conference of the International Law Association (1924), pp. 262, *et seq.*

[7] Projet d'une reglementation des voies de communications maritimes en temps de paix, Report of 33rd Conference (1924), pp. 259, *et seq.*

Professor Alvarez, individually, proposed a substitute draft article (as Article 6) concerning islands and archipelagos:

> As to islands situated outside or at the outer limit of a State's territorial waters, a special zone of territorial waters shall be drawn around such islands according to the rules contained in Article 4. Where there are archipelagos the islands thereof shall be considered a whole, and the extent of the territorial waters laid down in Article 4 shall be measured from the islands situated most distant from the center of the archipelago.[8]

The territorial-seas limit article (referred to as Article 4, in the above-quote article) suggested a zone of six nautical miles measured from low water marks. No maximum baseline distance between the islands of an archipelago was suggested.

In 1926, the Association met in Vienna, and although the territorial waters of archipelagos was discussed, the draft convention, as amended by the conference, made no reference whatsoever to archipelagos.[9]

American Institute of International Law

The American Institute of International Law (1926), in its Project No. 10 (National domain), produced a draft similar to Professor Alvarez's discussion and thereby also failed to provide for a maximum distance between islands of an archipelago. Article 7 did state that:

> In case of an archipelago, the islands and keys composing it shall be considered as forming a unit and the extent of territorial waters referred to in article 5 shall be measured from the islands farthest from the center of the Archipelago.[10]

The Harvard Research in International Law

The Harvard Research in International Law (1929) proposed three draft conventions in anticipation of the first conference on the codification of international law; namely, Nationality, Responsibility of States and Territorial Waters.[11]

Article 7, thereof, did discuss isolated islands:

> ... the marginal sea around an island or around land exposed only at some stage of the tide is measured outward three miles therefrom in the same manner as from the mainland.[12]

[8] *Ibid.*, p. 266; as translated by Mr. Evensen, *op. cit.*, p. 9.

[9] Report of 34th Conference (1926), p. 40, *et seq.*

[10] Am. J.I.L., Spec. suppl. 20 (1926), pp. 318–319. "The Committee of the Institute of International Law designated ... for the codification of American international law, and of which the Executive Committee [including such distinguished members as Alejandro Alvarez, James Brown Scott, Luis Anderson, *et al.*] of the Institute forms a part, presents the following series of projects of conventions for the preparation of a code of public international law. Habana, February 25, 1925." *Ibid.*, p. 300.

[11] Am. J.I.L., Spec. suppl. 23 (1929), p. 241, *et seq.*

[12] *Ibid.*, p. 275.

The comments to Article 7 stated, in part:

> ... in any situation where islands are within six miles of each other the marginal sea will form one extended zone. No different rule should be established for groups of islands or archipelagos except if the outer fringe of islands is sufficiently close to form one complete belt of marginal seas.[13]

Thus, the contributions, if any, made by the private scientific and scholarly organizations were ancillary to the main problem confronting them; namely, regulation of territorial waters. All four private organizations did recognize the existence of coastal archipelagos and they attempted to set forth delimitations but they did not reach the basic problems at issue in this study.

There were two major international conferences[14] that attempted to (a) define the problem regarding archipelagos snd (b) set forth a solution to the delimitation problem of territorial waters of archipelagos, in general. The first of these international conferences occurred in 1930.

THE HAGUE CODIFICATION CONFERENCE 1930 (CONFERENCE FOR THE CODIFICATION OF INTERNATIONAL LAW, LEAGUE OF NATIONS)

The Preparatory Committee (appointed by the League of Nations in 1924 to prepare a conference for the codification of international law) submitted a questionnaire to governments containing the following question regarding territorial waters:

> A group of islands: how near must islands be to one another to cause the whole group to possess a single belt of territorial waters?[15]

Commenting on this questionnaire some thirty years later, Professor Max Sorenson suggested that this conception of an archipelago as a group of islands constituting one unit for the purpose of measuring the territorial sea raised certain questions:[16]

> 1. What is the greatest permissible distance between the islands at the circumference of the group?
> 2. Is there any maximum permissible distance between islands within the group,

[13] *Ibid.*, p. 276. Therefore, in its draft convention on territorial waters (Part III, The law of territorial waters, p. 241, *et seq*). The Harvard Research in International Law failed to present any provision for archipelagos.

[14] The Hague Codification Conference, 1930 (Conference for the Codification of International Law, League of Nations) and the Geneva Conference on the Law of the Sea, 1958.

[15] Conference for the Codification of International Law, Bases of Discussion, vol. II, Territorial waters (Geneva, 1929), League of Nations Doc. C.74. M.39. 1929 V., p. 104.

[16] Sorenson, The territorial sea of archipelagoes, 6 Neth. I.L.R. (1959). Professor Sorenson's article was published in 1959 and will be discussed in this chapter, *infra*.

even in cases where the distance between islands at the circumference does not exceed the permissible maximum?

3. What is the status of the waters between the islands?

The questionnaire did, in fact, raise certain questions and they were placed into the framework of a basis of discussion (i.e., Basis of discussion no. 13) which stated that:

In the case of a group of islands which belong to a single State and at the circumference of the group are not separated from one another by more than twice the breadth of territorial waters, the belt of territorial waters shall be measured from the outermost islands of the group. Waters included within the group shall also be territorial waters.

The same rule shall apply as regards islands which lie at a distance from the mainland not greater than twice the breadth of territorial waters.[17]

Therefore, the substance of these questions, later raised by Professor Sorenson, was recognized at the Conference and was discussed, but few of the questions were answered at the Conference itself.

This reformulation as a basis of discussion proposal answered Professor Sorenson's three questions (in his opinion), as follows: question two was answered, by implication, in the negative;[18] questions one and three were answered in Basis of discussion No. 13 which provided for (1) a distance of not greater than twice the breadth of the territorial sea and (2) that the waters would be considered territorial.

The Preparatory Committee which dealt with territorial waters referred the item to its Second Sub-Committee of the Second Committee of the Conference. Since the twelve members of the Committee were prepared to propose a distance of ten miles, they submitted a ten-mile territorial zone limit. They submitted an archipelagic proposal to the Conference which read:

With regard to a group of islands (archipelago) and islands situated along the coast, the majority of the subcommittee was of the opinion that a distance of ten miles should be adopted as a basis for measuring the territorial sea outward in the direction of the high sea . . ..

The subcommittee did not express any opinion with regard to the nature of the waters included within the group.[19]

However, no precise draft article was formulated on archipelagos.

Nevertheless, in the amended draft convention on territorial waters prepared by Dr. Walther Schucking and the Committee of Experts, Article 5, paragraph 2, provided that:

[17] Am. J.I.L., Spec. suppl. 24 (1930), p. 34.

[18] However, it defies the imagination to locate a mid-ocean island group on this planet where the distance at the circumference does not, in fact, exceed the permissible maximum.

[19] Report of the Second Commission; League of Nations Document, C-230, M-117, 1930 V., p. 13.

In the case of archipelagos, the constituent islands are considered as forming a whole and the widths of the territorial sea shall be measured from the islands most distant from the center of the archipelago.[20]

Although the Conference discussed the possibility of treating certain island units as a whole, no formula was developed and the entire matter was discarded. It is significant that no maximum distance between the islands in an archipelago was proposed in Article 5(2).

Article 5, paragraph 1, contained provisions regarding coastal archipelagos:

If there are natural islands ... situated off the coast, the inner zone of the sea shall be measured from these islands, except in the event of their being so far distant from the mainland that they would not come within the zone of territorial sea if such zone were measured from the mainland ...[21]

No distinction was recognized between the problems applicable to coastal archipelagos and mid-ocean archipelagos.

No article was drafted on the subject because of arguments between the States concerning the matter of whether each island should have its own territorial waters or whether archipelagos should be treated as one unit. In addition, the States discussed delimitation problems but failed to distinguish between coastal and mid-ocean archipelagos. Not having dealt with the problem of territorial waters of archipelagos at the committee level, they certainly did not discuss, let alone analyze, the problem at the plenary sessions of the Conference.

Before examining the preparatory works submitted by the International Law Commission, and the Geneva Law of the Sea Conference of 1958, it is important to recall that the *Anglo-Norwegian Fisheries* case[22] was decided in 1951. This seven-year time span was a period when the matter was, or should have been, influencing the thinking of many representatives at the Conference, as it so clearly influenced the work of the International Law Commission,[23] regarding its application to coastal archipelagos and possibly to mid-ocean archipelagos, as well. This decision does not discuss the archipelagic-State concept but is important because of its holding in connection with measuring baselines.[24] It recognizes a system of baselines employed by Norway, some of which exceed 40 miles in length[25] along the Norwegian coast, and distinguishes

[20] League of Nations Doc.; C-196, M-70, 1927, V., p. 72; Am. J.I.L., Spec. suppl. 20 (1926), p. 142.

[21] *Ibid.*, the same pages.

[22] I.C.J. Reports 116 (1951).

[23] The influence of the thinking of various governments on the International Law Commission is discussed, *infra*, footnote 43.

[24] See Chapter II, *supra*, for its applicability to baseline delimitation.

[25] The total length of baselines is 645.90 nautical miles. There are 48 basepoints and 47 segments. The longest segment is 43.6 miles; the shortest segment is less than one mile and the

between coastal and mid-ocean archipelagos. However, the adjudication left open the question of whether a system of straight baselines can be applied to mid-ocean archipelagos. As alluded to in an earlier chapter[26] the criteria to be applied in choosing baselines was taken from the *Anglo Norwegian Fisheries* case, was later adopted by the Geneva Conference on the Law of the Sea, 1958, and is incorporated in Article 4, Convention on the Territorial Sea and Contiguous Zone.

Before assessing the preparatory work to the 1958 Law of the Sea Conference, a few comments by Jens Evensen as to the quality of that research and to the resulting draft articles are appropriate.[27]

The "factors ... invoked by coastal States ..." also extended from geographical, economical, historical and political factors, to include rationale by the archipelagic States in order to justify their unilateral declarations[28] regarding what the principal maritime States considered as traditionally high-seas waters.

The second point demonstrated by Jens Evensen was that although "the difficulties in trying to establish a *single* formula of fixed rules ..." (emphasis added) were evident to the International Law Commission,[29] they adhered to the traditional terms and governing concepts in order to formulate workable solutions regarding mid-ocean archipelagos. This rigidity characterizes all of the preparatory work of the International Law Commission and it may explain the fact that no reference to mid-ocean archipelagos appears in the end result of that preparatory work (i.e., the four conventions).

PREPARATORY WORK OF THE INTERNATIONAL LAW COMMISSION[30]

Article 10 of the First report (1952)[31] contained the following provision:

---

average segment is 11.9 miles. These figures were prepared and presented by two American geographers, Robert Hodgson and Lewis M. Alexander in: Towards an objective analysis of special circumstances, Occasional paper no. 13 (Law of the Sea Institute, Univ. of Rhode Island) (April, 1972), Appendix 1, p. 43.

[26] See Chapter II, *supra*.

[27] See: Jens Evensen, Certain legal aspects concerning the delimitation of the territorial waters of archipelagoes. A review of this document appears in this chapter, *infra*. The comments are set forth in Appendix A.

[28] See Chapter VI, *infra*, for a complete discussion of the declarations and significance thereof.

[29] This reference to a "single formula" should be kept in mind when considering the solution offered (Chapter VII, *infra*) in order to resolve the problem being presented herein.

[30] This discussion includes all of the relevant preparatory work for the 1958 Geneva Conference on the Law of the Sea which was conducted under the direction of Professor J. P. A. Francois (Special Rapporteur of the International Law Commission on Law of the Sea). The Commission's work was reported annually to the General Assembly of the United Nations in what are hereinafter referred to as first, second, third and subsequent reports.

[31] I.L.C., Fourth session, Report on the regime of the territorial sea, by J. P. A. Francois, Special Rapporteur. A/CN. 4/53 (1952).

With regard to a group of islands (archipelago) and islands situated along the coast, the ten-mile line shall be adopted as the baseline for measuring the territorial sea outward in the direction of the high sea. The waters included within the group shall constitute inland waters.[32]

Significantly, the article applied without distinction to "groups of islands (archipelagos)" and "islands situated along the coast." In addition, the draft article provided that baselines of not more than 10 miles be adopted for measuring territorial sea outward in the direction of the high sea. Waters in the group would be inland waters. Article 10 was later modified due to proposals made by a group of technical experts.[33]

Article 5, paragraph 2 of the First report (1952), concerning baselines, stated in part:

Nevertheless where a coast is deeply indented or cut into, or where it is bordered by an archipelago, the baseline becomes independent of the low water mark and the method of baselines joining appropriate points on the coasts must be employed . . . .[34]

However, in the Second report (1953), Article 5, paragraph 2 was amended, in part, apparently due to the holding in the *Anglo-Norwegian Fisheries* (1951) case:

As an exception where circumstances necessitate a special regime because the coast is deeply indented or cut into, or because there are islands in its immediate vicinity, the baseline may be independent of the low water mark . . . .[35]

Article 10 (as amended) of the Second report (1953), provided a ten mile maximum for baselines drawn between islands of an archipelago:

With regard to a group of islands (archipelago) and islands situated along the coast the ten mile line shall be adopted as the baseline.[36]

The intent of this amendment is clear, namely, to limit the situations where islands could be grouped together as one unit. The method employed was the adoption of a ten-mile baseline. However, it was recognized by Professor Francois that Article 10 of the First report[37] and this amendment were not in accord with the governing principles of international law as set forth by the Inter-

[32] *Ibid.*, p. 29.

[33] See amended Article 10, *infra*. The experts had proposed that in order that they might be regarded as constituting a group, the maximum distance between islands should be 5 miles instead of 10 except that in one case it might extend to 10. See Addendum to the Second report on the regime of the territorial sea, Annex report of the Committee of Experts on Technical Questions concerning the Territorial Sea, pp. 1–7. International Law Commission, Fifth Session, A/CN. 4/61 (1953).

[34] I.L.C., Fourth Session, *op. cit.*, p. 21.

[35] Addendum to the Second report on the regime of the territorial sea . . ., p. 30.

[36] *Ibid.*, p. 39.

[37] I.L.C., Fourth Session, *op. cit.*, p. 29.

national Court of Justice in the *Anglo-Norwegian Fisheries* case. Professor Francois stated, however, that the draft article was being submitted as a basis of discussion should the International Law Commission wish to study a text which envisaged the progressive development of international law on this subject.[38]

Article 9 of the Second report (1953), contained a proposal regarding isolated islands:

Every island has its own territorial sea. An island is an area of land surrounded by water, which is permanently above high water mark.[39]

Article 10 of the Second report (1953) was expanded and became Article 12 of the Third report (1954) and provided:[40]

1. The term "groups of islands," in the juridicial sense, shall be determined to mean three or more islands enclosing a portion of the sea when joined by straight lines not exceeding five miles in length, except that one such line may extend to a maximum of ten miles.
2. The straight lines specified in the preceeding paragraph shall be the base-lines for measuring the territorial sea. Waters lying within the area bounded by such lines and the islands themselves shall be considered as inland waters.
3. A group of islands may likewise by formed by a string of islands taken together with a portion of the mainland coastline. The rules set forth in paragraphs 1 and 2 of this Article shall apply *pari passu*.

This draft article first defined the term "group of islands," as three or more islands enclosing a portion of the sea when joined by straight lines not exceeding five miles in length, except that one such line may extend to a maximum of ten miles. There was no indication in the report as to how the five and ten-mile distances were arrived at except that they probably took the figures used by the Committee of Experts (which were never intended to be applicable to mid-ocean archipelagos)[41] regarding waters enclosed by arcs of islands to a bay. The draft article did not contain any provision for the

[38] International Law Commission, Fifth Session, A/CN. 4/61 (1953), p. 40. The comments stated that "The Rapporteur has inserted article 10 not as expressing the law at present in force, but as a basis of discussion should the Commission wish to study a text envisaging the progressive development of international law on the subject." This study is no place for a discussion of the relative performance of these assigned functions. It can be said that the problem herein is said to fall within progressive development rather than codification.

[39] *Ibid.*, p. 37. As will be alluded to throughout this book, the U.S. and other maritime nations still adhere to the view that each island shall have its own territorial sea, regardless of whether the islands form an archipelago or not, thereby excluding recognition of the treatment of archipelagic States as one unit.

[40] International Law Commission, 5th Session, Third report on the regime of the territorial sea, by J. P. A. Francois, Special Rapporteur, A/CN. 4/77 (1954), p. 13.

[41] The comments to Article 12 (Groups of Islands) stated: "Sub-Committee II of the 1930 Conference abandoned the idea of drafting a text on this subject. The Committee of Experts endeavored to provide also for this case. In drafting the article, the rapporteur followed the Committee's suggestion." *Ibid.*, p. 13.

maximum permissible distance between islands within the group, as distinct from the distance at the circumference. Thus, there was no limitation as to the areas of water which could be enclosed within the baselines. Paragraph 2 of the draft article provided that straight baselines between the islands should be the baselines for measuring the territorial sea. Waters within the area bounded by these lines and the islands should be considered inland waters.

The Commission did not draft any provision on groups of islands during the Seventh Session of the International Law Commission, 1955.[42] Professor Francois had explained that a limitation of the length of baselines between groups of islands was necessary in order to safeguard freedom of the sea and to prevent large areas of the sea from being enclosed as internal waters. In this regard, he had recommended that the length of the one "maximum" line be increased to 25 miles (apparently in order to conform with the same figure of 25 miles that was used by the Commission as a maximum length of a bay's closing line) while maintaining the other lines at five. However, members of the International Law Commission could not reach agreement on the text of an article regarding groups of islands.[43] The International Law Commission was finally coming to grips with the problem of groups of islands but notably in terms of baselines and other traditional concepts as applicable to coastal archipelagos. It does not appear that they were thinking in terms of mid-ocean archipelagos. They were not willing to accept Professor Francois' finding and they adjourned this discussion until the following year.

On the other hand, Article 5 permitted straight baselines, in part:

> ... where circumstances necessitate a special regime because the coast is deeply indented or cut into, or because there are islands in its immediate vicinity. . . .[44]

As was seen in the case of groups of islands, Article 5 was applicable to coastal archipelagos only and did not fix any maximum length for baselines. Article 5 also assumed that such waters inside the baselines were internal.

[42] United Nations General Assembly official records, Tenth Session, Supp. No. 9 (A/2934) entitled: Report of the International Law Commission, Seventh Session, 2 May–8 July, 1955.

[43] A summary of the discussion that took place at the 319th meeting is located in the Yearbook of the International Law Commission, vol. I, A/CN. 4/Ser. A/1955 319th meeting held June 24, 1955, pp. 217–218, paragraphs 57–66. One of the basic problems that could not be resolved was set forth by Mr. Garcia Amador: "The Commission should be consistent . . . it was difficult to see how an archipelago which was linked to the mainland by the geographical, economic or other ties which the International Court of Justice had considered relevant could now be severed from it on the ground that the islands of which it was composed were more than 5 miles apart, simply because the Committee of Experts had so recommended." *Ibid.*, p. 218, paragraph 61. Mr. Sandstrom and Sir Gerald Fitzmaurice also thought that perhaps it would be impossible to cover two different kinds of case in a single article. Sir Gerald Fitzmaurice stated, in part: "The whole idea of having special provisions for groups of islands was in order that the enclosed waters might be regarded as internal waters. The islands must therefore be reasonably close together." *Ibid.*, Summary records of the Seventh Sess., 2 May–8 July 1955, p. 218, paragraph 64.

[44] United Nations General Assembly official records, p. 82.

The problem of archipelagos was reviewed by the Eighth Session of the International Law Commission (1956).[45] In this final review of the draft articles relating to the territorial sea the International Law Commission recognized the principal problem of delimitation; namely, what was a group of islands? Widely scattered groups of islands with very extensive interior distance represent a very different situation from cases where islands are closely grouped, thus constituting more of a geographical and political unity. In cases where islands are closely grouped, it was thought that a special regime might be established, but a maximum distance between the islands and also a maximum distance of the interior lines would have to be adopted.[46]

In any event, in the final draft,[47] the International Law Commission again failed to present any specific provision regarding archipelagos and stated that it:

> . . . was prevented from stating an opinion, not only by disagreement on the breadth of the territorial sea, but also by lack of technical information on the subject.[48]

It may be observed that "lack of technical information" is a euphemism for lack of willingness to force the issue to some agreed statement. This want of incentive could be attributed to the fact that none of the post-World War II States was asserting, as yet, special adaptation of the law for their territorial water problems. Also, the leading maritime-law-making States had, themselves, been for centuries metropolitan States with archipelagic territories and had always accepted the one-island/separate-territorial-waters practice.

In this connection, Article 10 of the final draft, therefore, referred to isolated islands only:

> Every island has its own territorial sea. An island is an area of land, surrounded by water, which in normal circumstances is permanently above high water mark.[49]

In commenting on Article 10, the International Law Commission made statements concerning archipelagos:

> The Commission had intended to follow up this article with a provision concerning groups of islands. Like the Hague Conference for the Codification of International Law

[45] Yearbook of International Law Commission (1956), vol. II, p. 270. Report of I.L.C. to G.A. covering the work of its 8th Sess., 23 April–4 July 1956, p. 253, *et seq.*

[46] In this regard, there can exist a geographic situation where an archipelago may consist of one or more States. Also, there are countries (e.g., United Kingdom, Japan, Australia, etc.) which are archipelagos, geographically, but which are not considered as such historically. The applicability of these two situations to the problem being presented is discussed more fully in Chapter VII, *infra.*

[47] "Articles concerning the law of the sea" adopted by the International Law Commission in 1956.

[48] This comment regarding archipelagos is located after Article 10 (isolated islands), Yearbook of the International Law Commission (1956), vol. II, p. 270.

[49] *Ibid.*, p. 270.

of 1930 the Commission was unable to overcome the difficulties involved. *The problem is similarly complicated by the different forms it takes in different archipelagos.* The Commission was also prevented from stating an opinion, not only by disagreement on the breadth of the territorial sea, but also by lack of technical information on the subject. . . .[50] (Emphasis added.)

Article 5 of the final draft provided for the use of straight baselines:

Where circumstances necessitate a special regime because the coast is deeply indented or cut into, or because there are islands in its immediate vicinity.[51]

In commenting on Article 5, the International Law Commission made statements concerning coastal archipelagos:

4. The Commission points out for purposes of information that Article 5 may be applicable to groups of islands lying off the coast.[52]

Thus, the preparatory groundwork (which took the form of draft proposals) was completed by the International Law Commission on a note of discord concerning mid-ocean archipelagos.

GENEVA CONFERENCE ON THE LAW OF THE SEA, 1958

The draft proposals of the International Law Commission were adopted as a working basis of discussion at the Conference.[53]

At the outset of the Conference, Yugoslavia and the Philippines offered fresh initiatives.[54] Neither of which stipulated any specific limitations upon the method of delimitation that might be adopted in treating the group as one unit. Both proposals were withdrawn before being debated or voted upon by the First Committee of the Conference. The Yugoslavian proposal was reintroduced by a representative of the Danish delegation[55] but he later withdrew the proposal after statements made by Sir Gerald Fitzmaurice[56] suggested that the matter required further study.

No other fresh proposals or amendments to the proposals of the International Law Commission were offered nor were any solutions reached at the Conference. The main reason for this lack of accomplishment can be attributed

[50] *Ibid.*, p. 270 (Documents of the Eighth Session including the report of the Commission to the General Assembly).

[51] *Ibid.*, p. 257.

[52] *Ibid.*, p. 270.

[53] The study was intended for the United Nations Conference on the Law of the Sea to be held pursuant to General Assembly resolution 1105 (XI) of February 21, 1957 (Official record of the G.A., Eleventh Sess., Suppl. No. 17 (A/3572), p. 54). See Appendix A-1.

[54] UN Conf. on LOS, Off. rec., vol. III, pp. 227 and 239. A/CONF. 13/C. 1/L. 59 and 98. The Philippine and Yugoslavian proposals are set forth in Appendix A-2.

[55] See Appendix A-3. (UN Conf. on LOS, Off. rec., vol. III, p. 162.)

[56] *Ibid.*, p. 162.

to the emergence at the working level, and development in the conference, of what had by then become two diametrically opposed viewpoints.[57] On the one hand, Indonesia (the principle spokesman for the archipelagic States) believed that an archipelago should be treated as a single unit, the territorial sea of which should be measured from baselines drawn between the outermost islands. The waters situated to the interior of the baselines would be regarded as internal.[58] To the contrary, the United States (an active spokesman for the maritime nations) argued against this method of measuring the territorial sea:

> If you lump islands into an archipelago and utilize a straight baseline system connecting the outermost points of such islands and then draw a twelve-mile area around the entire archipelago, you unilaterally attempt to convert into territorial waters or possibly even internal waters vast areas of the high seas formerly freely used for centuries by the ships of all countries.[59]

Having reviewed the working proposals of the private scientific and scholarly organizations and discussed the suggestions set forth at the Hague Conference of 1930, the preparatory work of the International Law Commission and at the 1958 Law of the Sea Conference held in Geneva, it is necessary to review, as evidence of customary international law, relevant treaties, legislative and executive decrees, declarations and the practice of States regarding the treatment of mid-ocean archipelagos. This discussion will demonstrate that this evidence establishes that there is no degree of uniformity with regard to the delimitation problem as presented in this study.

CUSTOMARY INTERNATIONAL LAW

No consensus has been arrived at for any particular system of delimiting the bounds of authority over the waters of mid-ocean archipelagic islands and there is therefore no relevant rule on the nature of mid-ocean archipelagic waters.

TREATIES AS EVIDENCE OF CUSTOMARY INTERNATIONAL LAW

The method of treating an archipelago as one unit has not been consecrated in the treaty law. For example, in the treaties involving the Philippines and Northern Borneo, the wording refers to the islands (i.e., land territory), not to

[57] A complete discussion of the "special-general interests" dichotomy appears in Chapters VI, VII, *infra*.

[58] During the general debate, the representative of the Philippines (Mr. Arreglado) expressed similar views. See UN Conf. on LOS, Off. rec., vol. IV, p. 7. Cf., Yearbook of the International Law Commission, 1956, vol. II, p. 70. The comment of the Indonesian delegate is clearly further to, and consistent with, the unilateral declarations and guidelines that are discussed, *infra*, Chapter VI.

[59] U.S. Delegation to United Nations Conference on the Law of the Sea, Press release 3, March 11, 1958. Cf., UN Conf. on LOS, Off. rec., vol. III, pp. 25–27 (as taken from Sorenson, The territorial sea of archipelagos).

the areas of water within the specified lines.

Turning first to the Philippines, the treaty of peace between the United States and Spain, signed in Paris on December 10, 1898, provided in article 3 that:

> Spain cedes to the United States the archipelago known as the Philippine islands lying within the following lines.. . .[60]

After this wording, there follows a system of lines defined by various parallels of latitude and meridians of longitude.

With regard to the treaty involving Northern Borneo, the same method was applied in the Convention of January 2nd, 1930 between the United Kingdom and the United States concerning the boundary between the Philippines and Northern Borneo. Article 3 provides that:

> all islands to the north and east of the said line (laid down by art. 1) . . . shall belong to the Philippine Archipelago, and all islands to the south and west of the said line shall belong to the State of North Borneo.[61]

With regard to the interpretation of these articles, Professor Max Sorenson states that:[62]

> It seems quite clear that these treaties refer to the islands, that is the land territory, and not to the areas of the sea within the specified lines. This manner of defining the boundaries by longitudes and latitudes may have been the only practical method in view of the immense number of islands and could not be interpreted as revealing any intention to make provisions for the intervening waters outside what would otherwise be the ordinary limits of territorial waters.

LEGISLATIVE AND EXECUTIVE DECREES, DECLARATIONS AND THE PRACTICE OF STATES

The methods of straight baselines has been applied explicitly to archipelagos. For example, the Ecuadorian decree of February 21, 1951, relating to territorial waters, delimits in Article 3, the territorial sea around the Colon Archipelago (i.e., Galapagos Islands).[63] Indonesia and the Philippines have made similar declarations[64] and many countries protested this action on the ground that too much discretion was left to the archipelagic State.

Contrary to the above viewpoints, the United States treatment of the Colon Archipelago is the typical response and attitude of the maritime nations:

[60] 4 Whiteman digest of international law, p. 286 (British and foreign state papers, 1897–98, vol. XC, p. 382).

[61] League of Nations treaty series, vol. CXXXVII (137), p. 297 (as taken from 4 Whiteman digest of international law, pp. 286–287).

[62] The territorial sea of archipelagos, 6 Neth. I.L.R. (1959).

[63] U.N. leg. series, Laws and regulations on the regime of the territorial sea, 1957, p. 13. Other examples of state practice are discussed, *supra*, Chapter III.

[64] A complete discussion of these declarations and protests thereto is located in Chapter VI, *infra*.

The United States has, in common with the great majority of other maritime nations long adhered to the principle that the belt of territorial waters extends three marine miles from the coasts. This principle, when applied to insular possessions, contemplates a separate belt of territorial waters for each island, excepting where the water distance is less than six marine miles. Both the purported establishment of a belt of Ecuadorian territorial waters twelve nautical miles in breadth, and the assertion of a claim to a single belt of territorial waters around the entire Colon Archipelago, contravene this principle of international law.[65]

The legislation extending the application of treaties, likewise, establishes no firm evidence of customary state practice.

PUBLICISTS AND LEGAL WRITERS USUALLY STATE THE PROBLEM IN TRADITIONAL TERMS

From the earliest references in the writings of the publicists to the subject of this book and ever since 1958 and up to the present date, the publicists and legal writers have attempted to define and resolve the problem of mid-ocean archipelagos by applying the traditional terms and governing concepts which have bedeviled an accurate treatment of the problem from the beginning. In order to understand the limitations and complexities of the traditional legal terms and governing concepts confronting the publicists and the legal writers that attempt to deal with the law of territorial waters of archipelagic States, it is necessary to examine the considerations involved. The elementary consideration for the writers when arguing against the application of the straight baseline system is related to the legal status of the waters enclosed by such baselines. In other words, do the waters become "internal" and therefore subject to the highest degree of jurisdictional competence? A second persistent consideration has been the question of the freedom of navigation and all of the other freedoms finally embodied in the Convention on the High Seas. The waters located between the islands will often have the character of straits connecting two parts of the "high seas"; and, if the waters between the islands had previously been high seas, all of the freedoms provided for in Article 2 of the Convention on the High Seas would be eliminated.

A third elementary consideration involves the length of baselines that could be permissible. Short baselines could enclose large areas of high seas where the distance between islands at the circumference is small and where the distance between islands inside the archipelago is wide. In archipelagos, the islands could be separated by what would be areas of high seas if no other method was applied where some or all distances between neighboring islands at the perimeter as well as inside the group exceed the double breadth of the territorial sea.

[65] Note of protest dated June 7, 1951; quoted from I.C.J. *Anglo-Norwegian Fisheries* case, I.C.J. reports 116 (1951), Pleadings, etc., vol. IV, p. 604.

With these considerations in mind, it is now possible to review, briefly, the works of various publicists and legal writers.

The first full discussion and certainly also the most original and thorough article was prepared by Jens Evensen (1958) at the request of the Secretariat of the United Nations[66] for the 1958 Conference on the Law of the Sea. The study contained a complete discussion of archipelagos and distinguished between the treatment that was afforded to coastal and mid-ocean archipelagos.[67] Mr. Evensen attempts to resolve the delimitation problem regarding mid-ocean archipelagos, by utilizing an analogy to the *Anglo-Norwegian Fisheries* case. He combined the criteria of that case[68] with traditional terms and governing concepts[69] that had been applied to coastal archipelagos. His main contribution as far as this thesis is concerned is that he recognized the difficulties in attempting to create a "single formula of fixed rules"[70] regarding the delimitation of the territorial waters of archipelagos. He recognized the fact that "no hard and fast rules exist whereby a State is compelled to disregard the geographical, historical (and economical) peculiarities of outlying archipelagos."[71]

Thereafter, Mr. Evensen proposed a treaty article based upon the foregoing criteria:

1. In the case of an archipelago which belongs to a single State and which may reasonably be considered as a whole, the extent of the territorial sea shall be measured from the outermost points of the outermost islands and islets of the archipelago. Straight baselines as provided for under Article 5 may be applied for such delimitation.

2. The waters situated between and inside the constituent islands and islets of the archipelago shall be considered as internal waters with the exceptions set forth under paragraph 3 of this article.

3. Where the waters between and inside the islands and islets of an archipelago form a strait, such waters cannot be closed to the innocent passage of foreign ships.[72]

Mr. Evensen believed that while straight baselines could be used for delimiting territorial waters of an archipelago that is "looked upon as a whole,"[73] it is possible to use methods other than straight baselines such as arcs of circles. He stated further that waters located between and inside the islands and islets of this type of archipelago "must"[74] be treated as internal waters. The only excep-

[66] Certain legal aspects concerning the delimitation of the territorial waters of archipelagoes, U.N. Doc. A/CONF. 13/18, U.N. Conference on the Law of the Sea, Preparatory documents 1958 (1958), vol. I.

[67] The concept of archipelagic States was not reviewed because it was not in existence at that time. The concept, itself, is a proposal devised by the one-unit theorists.

[68] The criteria are set forth, *supra*, Chapter II.

[69] See Chapter II.

[70] Certain legal aspects concerning the delimitation of the territorial waters of archipelagoes, p. 5.

[71] *Ibid.*, pp. 36 and 37. See Appendix A-4.

[72] *Ibid.*, pp. 37 and 38.

[73] *Ibid.*, p. 38.

[74] *Ibid.*

tion would be where the waters formed a strait, because of the prevailing rules of international law that prevented closing a strait to traffic.

Mr. Evensen was the first legal writer to treat mid-ocean archipelagos as one unit. There were certain international law publicists, before Mr. Evensen prepared his article, who considered that coastal archipelagos could be considered as one unit. However, the viewpoints stated by these publicists are usually brief statements or general observations. For example, Jessup (in 1927),[75] without distinguishing between coastal and mid-ocean archipelagos, urged adoption of the following rule:

In the case of archipelagos the constituent islands are considered as forming a unit and the extent of territorial waters is measured from the islands farthest from the center of the archipelagos.

So also Hyde (1947):[76]

Where, however, a group of islands forms a fringe or cluster around the ocean front of a maritime State it may be doubted whether there is evidence of any rule of international law that obliges such State invariably to limit or measure its claims to the waters around them by the exact distance which separate the several units.

Again, Schwarzenberger argued (in 1949) that there may be certain circumstances where archipelagos could be regarded as a unit in law.[77] He later stated (in 1957) that in the case of archipelagos, the establishment of a territorial jurisdiction is a gradual process.[78]

The French jurist Gidel stated (in 1934),[79] with reference to coastal archipelagos, that they could be treated as a unit if a maximum of ten nautical miles for the baselines between the islands and islets of the group or between the mainland and the nearest island of the group was established. Only "the theory of historic waters"[80] would justify longer lengths of baselines. He suggested that the waters lying between the islands forming the archipelago or between the archipelago and the mainland should be considered as territorial, not internal, in nature. Gidel's suggestion regarding mid-ocean archipelagos is to be found in his discussion of ten-mile baselines:[81]

In the case of an archipelago situated far from land (mid-ocean archipelago) the measuring of territorial waters must be made in conformity with the ordinary rules, individually around each island; exceptions to these rules may follow from the theory of

[75] The law of territorial waters and maritime jurisdiction (New York, 1927), pp. 457 and 477.

[76] International law, 2nd ed., vol. I (Boston, 1947), p. 485.

[77] International law, vol. I (1949), p. 156.

[78] International law, vol. I (1957), p. 336.

[79] Le droit international public de la mer (The public international law of the sea), vol. III (Paris, 1934), pp. 706–727.

[80] *Ibid.*, p. 724.

[81] *Ibid.*, p. 718; translation obtained from Mr. Evensen, Certain legal aspects concerning the delimitation of the territorial waters of archipelagoes.

historic waters. However, pockets of high seas inside the archipelago may be eliminated by the analogous application of the ten mile rule applicable to bays.

This suggestion clearly lacks the usual clarity of this great international law publicist.

Other international legal publicists favoring the treatment of a coastal archipelago as one unit are two Argentine writers, namely, Podesta Coasa[82] and Diez Cisneros.[83]

Thus far, it may be observed that the treatment of coastal archipelagos as one unit was generally favored provided that a maximum distance for the length of baselines was established. Nevertheless, in the late 1950s and early 1960s there suddenly appeared a few law review articles (all published within a couple of years of each other, and possibly, not coincidentally, at or around the same time as the unilateral declarations of the Philippines and Indonesia) calling for the applicability of similar one-unit treatment to mid-ocean archipelagos that were independent States. And so there emerged the development of the archipelagic-State concept based upon traditional terms and governing concepts that were never intended to be employed in this area.

LEADING LAW REVIEW ARTICLES TREAT THE PROBLEM IN TRADITIONAL TERMS

The first article for discussion was written by Professor Max Sorenson in 1959.[84] After carefully reviewing the background materials, preparatory works of the International Law Commission and general history regarding the subject matter (including the lack of uniformity of State practice), he set forth as a basis for discussion an "either/or," polarized question placed in a traditional framework:

The question is whether it is permissible under international law to apply some system of straight baselines for the delimitation of the territorial sea of archipelagos, and if so in what conditions, or whether, alternatively, the outer limits of the territorial sea shall always be measured from the low-water mark on the islands, which would mean that each island has its own territorial sea to the extent that there is not overlapping of the territorial sea of neighbouring islands.[85]

Professor Sorenson recognized the existence of at least two main problems.

One of the considerations which have often been invoked against the application of the straight baselines system is related to the legal status of the waters enclosed by such baselines.[86]

[82] Derecho international publico (1955), p. 227.
[83] Derecho international publico, I., p. 530.
[84] The territorial sea of archipelagos.
[85] *Ibid.*, p. 324.
[86] *Ibid.*, p. 327.

As to this first problem, he stated that:

Proposals for applying this system to archipelagos have generally assumed that the areas of the sea, which were enclosed by the baselines, should have the status of internal waters, . . . However, the adverse effects which this solution might otherwise have had upon the freedom of navigation, are now obviated by the principle adopted by the Geneva Convention art. 5, paragraph 2, which seems applicable by analogy to the present problem.[87]

It will be recalled that Article 5 of the Convention on the Territorial Sea and the Contiguous Zone provides:

1. Waters on the landward side of the baseline of the territorial sea form part of the internal waters of the State.
2. Where the establishment of a straight baseline in accordance with article 4 has the effect of enclosing as internal waters areas which previously had been considered as part of the territorial sea or of the high seas, a right of innocent passage, as provided in articles 14 to 23, shall exist in those waters.[88]

Professor Sorenson is therefore drawing an analogy in the use of baselines as between coastal archipelagos (narrowly grouped together) and mid-ocean archipelagos (however scattered).

Professor Sorenson's recognition of the second problem brings him truly to grips with the essential difficulty of enclosing wide areas of traditional high-seas areas as internal waters. He also reaches the related problem of allowing mid-ocean archipelagic States to assert sovereignty over areas of high seas that may enormously exceed their total land mass:

The question remains what lengths of baselines should be permitted. In the case of outlying archipelagos this question assumes another significance than in the case of coastal archipelagos, because it must be considered in connection with the question of the interior distances between the islands. It may very well be that the distance between islands at the circumference is small but that distances between islands inside the archipelago are wide. Even short baselines may therefore in such circumstances enclose vast areas of the sea.

An extreme case, which is well suited to illustrate the point at issue, would exist if all distances between islands at the perimeter of a group were less than the double breadth of the territorial sea, but the distance at some of the diameters was many times that length because of the existence of a large 'internal sea'. In such a case the first question to be answered is what would be status of that 'internal sea' if straight baselines were not drawn. If it was part of the territorial sea, its status would remain practically unaffected by the drawing of straight baselines at the perimeter, because the transformation into internal waters would be tempered by the maintenance of a right of innocent

[87] *Ibid.*, p. 327.

[88] Convention adopted by the U.N. Conference on the Law of the Sea, April 29, 1958 (516 U.N. treaty series 205, Treaty No. I: 7477); 45 States have ratified as of October 28, 1974. See Chapter II, *supra*, for a discussion regarding Article 4 (i.e., baseline measurement for coastal archipelagos—the outgrowth of the *Anglo-Norwegian Fisheries* case) and Chapter II, *supra*, for a discussion of the right of innocent passage.

passage. If, on the other hand, it was part of the high seas, its status would be considerably modified, because a number of the freedoms pertaining to the high seas, in particular the freedom to fish, would be eliminated.[89]

Analagous to this problem, Professor Sorenson also raised the question which he considered to be ". . . the really controversial type of case,"[90] namely, the case of mid-ocean archipelagos belonging to the less compact type, ". . . where some or all distances between neighbouring islands at the perimeter as well as inside the group exceed the double breadth of the territorial sea so that the islands are separated by what would be areas of high seas if no other method was applied."[91] In this connection, Professor Sorenson believed that:

. . . If one only relied on art. 4 of the Convention regarding coastal archipelagos, and lines were consequently drawn between islands 40 or 50 miles apart at a perimeter which would allow even greater interior distances, the legal status of vast areas of the sea would be transformed. The freedoms of the high sea not least the right to fish, would be unreasonably interfered with, and the coastal state might not even be able effectively to exercise jurisdiction and control over such vast areas.[92]

Having recognized the difficulties of resolving the problem by using traditional legal terms, Professor Sorenson stated that:

The whole subject matter abounds with sources of international conflict and friction. An extended acceptance of compulsory adjudication seems to be the only way of compensating for the unsatisfactory state in which international law on this subject has been left despite repeated efforts of codification.[93]

Jurge R. Coquia, also writing in 1959,[94] agreed with Professor Sorenson in stating that there has never been a universal agreement as to the precise nature of a state's rights over those parts of the sea that wash their shores. Mr. Coquia stated that the problem of delimiting a territorial sea, in general, is affected by

. . . (1) The lack of generally accepted limits for the breadth of the territorial sea, (2) the lack of well developed and universally accepted techniques and principles for the delimitation of the territorial sea, (3) the tendency of State to protect national interests with a view of preserving and promoting particular economic, political and security interests, (4) the essentially unilateral character of the acts of delimitation due to its dependence upon the geographic, historical and economic circumstances of each State.[95]

[89] Convention, *ibid.*, p. 328.
[90] *Ibid.*, p. 329.
[91] *Ibid.*, p. 329.
[92] *Ibid.*, p. 329.
[93] *Ibid.*, p. 331.
[94] Participant, 1959, Centre for Studies and Research, Hague Academy of International Law, Peace Palace, The Hague. The article written by J. Coquia is entitled: The problem of the territorial waters of archipelagoes, 7 Far Eastern L. Rev. 435 (1959).
[95] *Ibid.*, pp. 435–436.

Mr. Coquia repeated the same "either/or" question posed in Professor Sorenson's article as a basis for discussion[96] and then defined an archipelago as: "An archipelago is a formation of two or more islands, (islets or creeks) which geographically may be considered as a whole."[97] Mr. Coquia proposed a method of approach toward obtaining a solution. That "juristic approach" was to apply the International Court of Justice approach in cases of apparent novelty on the ground that rules of international law do not exist.[98] Thus, the International Court of Justice would be entitled to proceed to an independent examination and solution to the problems involved. Mr. Coquia posed two questions for review, namely:

> ... do the special interests of the archipelagic States constitute sufficient reason for the adoption of a special rule for them?

and

> Are these special interests also adequate and justifiable under the general principles of international law?[99]

His response to his two questions commenced by stating:

> ... that an archipelago is a body of water studded with islands, rather than islands with waters ... the waters between and around them form part and parcel of the territory.[100]

The gravamen of the argument was that if the special interests of the archipelagic States were not protected by application of the one-unit concept, then "... the continuity of the jurisdiction of the government would thus be disrupted ...."[101]

Again, in 1961, the one-unit concept takes a central place in J.J.G. Syatauw's article which is incorporated into his book.[102] Throughout, Mr. Syatauw is concerned with the special interests of Indonesia (which are no

[96] *Ibid.*, p. 437.

[97] *Ibid.*, p. 437, misquoting Evensen's definition by using "creeks" instead of "rocks".

[98] The reference is to the use that the International Court of Justice made to the apparent novelty consideration in its advisory opinion bearing on the *Reservations to the Genocide Convention* (cited in Mr. Coquia's article as I.C.J. Reports 1951, p. 32). *Ibid.*, pp. 447–448.

[99] *Ibid.*, p. 453.

[100] *Ibid.*, p. 453. Mr. Coquia is making the same point that was made by Mr. Subardjo of the Indonesian delegation whereby he stated that "... an archipelago being essentially a body of water studded with islands rather than islands with water around them. ..." See U.N. Conf. on LOS, Off. rec., vol. III, Summary records of meetings and annexes, 15th Meeting held 14 March 1958, p. 43, paragraph 4.

[101] Mr. Coquia's article, *ibid.*, p. 453.

[102] Some newly established Asian States and the development of international law (The Hague: Martinus Nijhoff, 1961).

different than those of the Philippines, for example) and stated that Indonesia had been criticized for its transformation of extensive high-seas areas into internal waters.[103] However, he pointed out that the Indonesian declaration and legislation does concede "innocent passage" in internal waters if neither prejudicial to nor in violation of the sovereignty and security of Indonesia.[104] His only criticism is that such a view of "innocent passage" would "blur" the dividing line between internal and territorial waters, a distinction which has always been clearly distinguished by limiting the right of innocent passage to territorial waters.[105] In his discussion of archipelagic States, Mr. Syatauw fails to develop clearly that this blurring results in the archipelagic States having the final say as to the extent of innocent passage,[106] whereas before they did not sit in judgment.[107]

Mr. Syatauw accepts and justifies the one-unit concept of an archipelagic State by stating that a movement away from the shore is only truly in a direction away from the land-based territorial jurisdiction of the coastal State if the starting point of that movement is taken from the outer perimeter of the archipelago.[108] In addition, within the mid-ocean archipelago, any movement away from a land-based territorial jurisdiction is at the same time a movement closer to another jurisdiction which has its origin on the nearest land territory of the other islands or groups of islands adjacent to or near the perimeter of the mid-ocean archipelago.[109] In his view, the implications of this argument require that the waters lying within the unit should be considered "internal."[110] Therefore, he reaches the conclusion that all waters lying within the perimeter of an archipelagic State are not high seas.[111]

Mr. Syatauw agrees with Indonesia's argument that from time immemorial, her archipelago constituted one unit and that his general argument may therefore be buttressed by the consideration that Indonesia's intermediate waters are historic waters.[112] Despite all of Mr. Syatauw's arguments presented in support of the one-unit concept, he finally concludes:[113]

[103] A full discussion of the unilateral declarations of the Philippines and Indonesia appears in Chapter VI, *infra.*

[104] Some newly established Asian States . . ., p. 131.

[105] The right of innocent passage is discussed more fully in Chapter II, *supra.*

[106] Notice how various law of the sea terms are being erroded in order to fit solutions into existing conventional law.

[107] Some newly established Asian States . . ., p. 196.

[108] *Ibid.*

[109] *Ibid.*

[110] *Ibid.*

[111] *Ibid.*, p. 198.

[112] *Ibid.*, p. 199. It would seem that the use of the term "historic waters" is made by way of an analogy to the traditional concept of an historic bay. The analogy, however, is not fully argued. On the Indonesian government's utilization of his analogy and the concept generally of historic waters, see the proposals and comments thereon located, *infra*, Chapter V. The Dutch treatment of the Indonesian archipelago is discussed, *infra*, Chapter VII.

[113] Some newly established Asian States . . ., p. 200.

> ... the solution cannot lie in the creation of a *rigid* (emphasis added) rule for the future, but in the contemporary balancing of the exclusive national claims against the inclusive demands of a world community.

The language contained in this formula sets the stage for a discussion of the views of McDougal and Burke in their well known treatise, Public order of the oceans.[114] Contained within their extensive chapter regarding the delimitation of baselines is a rather limited discussion of the "claims" regarding mid-ocean ("non-adjacent")[115] archipelagos. The analysis of these "claims" is broken into a "clarification of policy," "trends in decision" and "appraisal and recommendation" and the contents thereof are set forth in terms of "factors" and "exclusive interests."[116]

In this context, it is stated that:[117]

> The important question for policy is whether any or all of these factors establish a need for comprehensive coastal authority over the adjoining ocean, as these states [mid-ocean archipelagic States] sometimes suggest, or whether more limited, specially designed zones of authority might adequately protect exclusive interest.

The use of the phrase "comprehensive coastal authority" carries an implication that the problem can be handled without directly utilizing the one-unit concept. Instead, they suggest the use of the low-water line of each island as an individual baseline thereby creating increased contiguous zone areas. Within these increased areas, it is contemplated that additional interests could be recognized.

Their approach places the burden of proof on the archipelagic State. In other words, before an archipelagic State can use increased contiguous zone areas and administer interests within such areas, it must show the need for such action. With respect to the burden of proof requirement, we have already noted in the earlier discussion of baseline delimitation,[118] that The Geographer of the U.S. Department of State compiled a list of states that employ one or more lines in excess of the 40-nautical-mile segment limit[119] which was recognised in the *Anglo-Norwegian Fisheries* case. In addition, non-archipelagic-type States need not prove any interest in their adjoining sea areas in order for treaty rights arising out of the 1958 conventions to accrue to them.[120]

There is a gap in the appearance of significant articles on the subject of mid-ocean archipelagos and archipelagic States from 1962 until Ambassador Amerasinghe's article appeared in the International and comparative law

[114] Public order of the oceans, p. 12.

[115] *Ibid.*, p. 411.

[116] *Ibid.*, pp. 411, 415 and 418.

[117] *Ibid.*, p. 419.

[118] See discussion located, *supra*, Chapter II.

[119] One nautical mile equals 6076.116 feet. This list is set forth, *supra*, Chapter II.

[120] These are some of the considerations that were dealt with when planning the proposal presented in this book.

quarterly, in 1974.[121] During this gap, the United Nations Sea-bed Committee was established in 1968, but it was not until its meeting in 1973 (Geneva) that its deliberations included a serious discussion of draft proposals regarding the mid-ocean archipelagic State problems.[122] However, no proposal was offered that could be considered workable because each proposal contained a misplaced reliance on traditional terms and governing concepts. As will be seen later, various approaches to the solution of the problem have been offered[123] (i.e., treatment of the archipelagic State as a special regime), but no viable recommendation was forthcoming.

Mr. C. F. Amerasinghe (currently serving as Legal Advisor to the International Bank for Reconstruction and Development) had closely followed these developments. His article, in 1974, was therefore noted with great interest.[124] It contains a rather extensive discussion of the problem, reviews the draft proposals at the United Nation Sea-bed Committee, as well as "recent alternative suggestions" proposed,[125] and contains a section on "prospects and approaches to solutions."[126] While a final solution is not offered, there is a strong suggestion that:[127]

> The best *approach* . . . is to treat mid-ocean archipelagoes as having a *special regime* in which the archipelagic State has, because of special considerations, special rights over and above what it would have had if a special regime had not been recognized, while other States and the international community also have some, though limited, rights in them . . .

[121] Other articles include: D. P. O'Connell, Mid-ocean archipelagos in international law, 45 Brit. Y.I.L. 1 (1973); J. J. G. Syatauw, Revisiting 'the archipelago': an old concept gains new respectability, 29 India quart. 104 (1973).

[122] The general Assembly first included an item concerning the peaceful uses of the seabed beyond national jurisdiction in its agenda during 1967. A complete history of the Committee can be found in: 1 Report of the Committee on the peaceful uses of the sea-bed and the ocean floor beyond the limits of national jurisdiction 1–12, U.N. off. rec.: G.A. 28th Sess. supp. no. 21 (A/9021) (1973).

[123] See Chapter V, *infra*.

[124] The problem of archipelagoes in the international law of the sea, 23 I.C.L.Q. 539 (Part 3) (1974).

[125] *Ibid.*, pp. 559–562.

[126] *Ibid.*, pp. 562–575.

[127] *Ibid.*, p. 575.

CHAPTER V

PROPOSED SOLUTIONS TO THE PROBLEM, IN GENERAL

Having reviewed all of the materials that contain any reference to mid-ocean archipelagos, archipelagic States and coastal archipelagos, and having observed the problems presented, in general, and the approaches to solutions offered, it is now important to review certain concrete solutions that were presented at the 1973 United Nations Sea-bed Committee meeting held in Geneva. The polarized positions of the "special-general interest" groups will become apparent.

At the outset, it may be observed that the preceding four chapters have each taken a different approach to the problem of this study.

In Chapter I, the traditional legal terms and governing concepts were analyzed at some length in order to prepare the basis for discussion. In Chapter II, the special problems arising from the use of these terms and concepts with respect to coastal archipelagos, fringe islands, artificial islands and structures, and offshore islands was set forth in order to serve as both an introduction to the problem and subject matter presented in this study and as a bridge to a full disclosure of the historical review presented in Chapter III. In Chapter III, after setting forth the contributions made by the private scientific and scholarly organizations, the 1930 and 1958 international conferences and the international publicists. The leading studies of Jens Evensen,[1] Max Sorenson,[2] Jurge R. Coquia,[3] J. J. G. Syatauw,[4] and C. F. Amerasinghe[5] were particularly reviewed as a means of assuring that every effort was made to reach all of the issues raised in the literature. However, it was observed that no formal proposals were submitted with respect to the mid-ocean archipelagos that, from 1958, were beginning to be referred to as "archipelagic States"; nor did the leading maritime nations take formal cognizance of the problem until after 1958. Consequently, there was no discussion concerning the arguments of the "special-general interest" groups. However, in 1973, at the two sessions of the

[1] Discussed, *supra*, Chapter IV.
[2] *Ibid.*
[3] *Ibid.*
[4] *Ibid.*
[5] *Ibid.*

United Nations Sea-bed Committee held in New York and Geneva[6] and at the 1974 Law of the Sea Conference in Caracas, formal national delegation proposals were made, and arguments were set forth, in the working documents. This chapter will discuss the arguments of the States concerning the formal proposals and, in particular, the two key diametrically opposed proposals of Indonesia, Philippines, Mauritius and the Fiji delegations on the one hand, and the United Kingdom, as spokesman for the general maritime nation interests. The arguments presented will help demonstrate the complexities of the problem and the particular interests sought to be protected as well as provide a basis for determining whether the proposal presented in Chapter VII would serve to resolve the problem presented now. As might be expected, all of the arguments arising from the formal proposals concern the delimitation problem as presented.

The formal proposal[7] by the delegations of Indonesia, Philippines, Mauritius and Fiji submitted at the 1973 United Nations Sea-bed Committee in Geneva was dated August 6, 1973. In March of the same year, these four States had set forth certain statements of guidelines. Therefore, these guidelines will be set forth, firstly.[8] Thereafter, the formal proposal of August 6, 1973 will be examined and compared with the March guidelines. Other States presented very limited proposals that did not vary the contents of the August 6, 1973 proposal.[9]

THE GUIDELINES OF THE ARCHIPELAGIC STATES, DATED MARCH 14, 1973[10]

1. An archipelagic State, whose component islands and other natural features form an intrinsic geographical, economic and political entity, and historically have or may have been regarded as such, may draw straight baselines connecting the outermost points of the outermost islands and drying reefs of the archipelago from which the extent of the territorial sea of the archipelagic State is or may be determined.

[6] The first session was held in New York from 5 March to April 6; the second session was held in Geneva from 2 July to August 24.

[7] An examination of this proposal was made by C. F. Amerasinghe in The problem of archipelagoes in the international law of the sea, 23 I.C.L.Q. 539 (Part 3) (1974).

[8] The considerations that are incorporated in the guidelines (this chapter, *infra*) and the proposal of the archipelagic states (this chapter, *infra*) have already been analyzed, *supra*, Chapter IV, and an interpretative analysis will be provided, *infra*, Chapter VI.

[9] See 4 Report of the Committee on the peaceful uses of the seabed and the ocean floor, U.N. off. rec.: 6.A. 28th Sess. supp. no. 21 (A/9021) (1973), pp. 156, *et seq.*; 3 *ibid.*, pp. 26, 41; and 6 *ibid.*, p. 106. Examples of these proposals are set forth in Appendix A-5.

[10] U.N. Doc. A/AC. 138/SC. II/L. 15. Submitted by the delegations of Fiji, Indonesia, Mauritius and the Philippines. The Explanatory Note contained in the guidelines disclosed that: "This paper is submitted by Fiji, Indonesia, Mauritius and the Philippines for consideration by this Committee with a view to the principles enunciated therein being incorporated into the convention on the law of the sea. These principles are designed to accommodate not only the interests of archipelagic States but also other States and of the international community as a whole. They contain the definition of an archipelagic State, its rights over the waters of the archipelago, and the right of innocent passage for international navigation through the waters of the archipelago."

2. The waters within the baselines, regardless of their depth or distance from the coast, the sea-bed or subsoil thereof, and the superjacent air space, as well as all their resources, belong to, and are subject to the sovereignty of the archipelagic State.

3. Innocent passage of foreign vessels through the waters of the archipelagic State shall be allowed in accordance with its national legislation, having regard to the existing rules of international law. Such passage shall be through sealanes as may be designated for that purpose by the archipelagic State.

The excellent summary (which does not pretend to be an analysis of these guidelines) by C. F. Amerasinghe, cannot be improved upon.[11]

THE FORMAL PROPOSAL OF THE ARCHIPELAGIC STATES, DATED AUGUST 6, 1973[12]

The formal proposal of August 6, 1973 revised somewhat the guidelines issued in March, 1973 and contained the archipelagic principles as set forth in Appendix C.

This formal proposal differed from the guidelines of March, 1973, and reference is made to the summary and list of said differences prepared by C. F. Amerasinghe:[13]

(i) it makes the historical factor an alternative to the other factors involved in the definition of an archipelago and not a cumulative factor;

(ii) it lays down as a requirement that the baselines should not depart to any appreciable extent from the general configuration of the archipelago;

(iii) it makes clear that low-tide elevations are not to be used as end-points for the drawing of baselines except where installations such as lighthouses which are permanently above sea level have been built on them or where a low-tide elevation is situated wholly or partly at a distance not exceeding the breadth of the territorial sea from the nearest island;

(iv) it specifically limits the drawing of baselines in such a way as not to cut off the territorial sea of another State, which means that priority is to be given to the determination of the territorial sea of other coastal States where the special regime for archipelagoes becomes applicable;

(v) due publicity is to be given to charts indicating the straight baselines after they are determined;

(vi) the right to designate sealanes for the passage of foreign vessels through the archipelagic waters within the straight-baselines is dealt with in greater detail. Particularly provision is made for:

(a) substitution of other sealanes for previously designated sealanes after due publicity has been given;

(b) the institution of traffic separation schemes for passage through the designated sealanes; and

[11] The problem of archipelagoes in the international law of the sea, pp. 548–549. See Appendix B.

[12] U.N. Doc. A/AC. 138/SC. II/L. 48. As stated, *supra*, in footnote 8, the considerations that are incorporated in the guidelines and the proposal of the archipelagic States (commencing on this page) have already been analyzed. and an interpretative analysis will be provided.

[13] The problem of archipelagoes ir the international law of the sea, pp. 551–552.

(c) the imposition by the archipelagic State of laws and regulations, subject to the provisions of the draft articles and other provisions of international law, relating to passage through the designated sealanes and traffic separation schemes;

(vii) the treatment of warships exercising the right of innocent passage is specifically dealt with;

(viii) suspension of innocent passage through designated sealanes is prohibited except (a) when essential for the security of the archipelagic State; (b) after due publicity has been given, and (c) after substitution of other sealanes.

THE UNITED KINGDOM PROPOSAL AS REPRESENTATIVE OF THE VIEWS OF THE GENERAL MARITIME STATES[14]

The diametrically opposed position of the general maritime States was submitted as a formal proposal by the United Kingdom of Great Britain and Northern Ireland as a draft article on the rights and duties of archipelagic States at the 1973 United Nations Sea-bed Committee meeting held in Geneva.

Obviously, this proposal defines the term "archipelagic State" by use of a definitional land/sea ratio with the consequent general restrictive effect over the waters regarded as internal waters and the withholding of jurisdiction over specific uses and resources in the high-seas areas. A summary of this proposal (but again not an analysis) has been set forth by C. F. Amerasinghe:[15]

> The main points of difference between the two proposals are that the U.K. proposal: (i) imposes limitations on the length of straight baselines drawn between islands—such length is not to exceed 48 nautical miles; (ii) no mention is made of a right to use low-tide elevations on which there are permanent installations as end-points for baselines; (iii) the territorial sea of another State is not explicitly protected against diminution by the drawing of baselines; (iv) the area of the waters enclosed by the baselines is limited to five times the area of the land territory within the perimeter; (v) the right of innocent passage granted to foreign vessels through the archipelagic waters would appear to be identical with that which exists for such vessels through the territorial sea; (vi) a right of passage similar to that which exists for foreign vessels through international straits is granted to foreign vessels through straits which would have been international straits had the archipelagic regime not been recognised.

The arguments of the States at the 1973 United Nations Sea-bed Committee meeting held in Geneva and the 1974 Law of the Sea Conference held in Caracas (a) highlight the differences of the two proposals and (b) help set forth the framework within which a compromise solution can be accomplished. Firstly, at the 1973 United Nations Sea-bed Committee meeting (Geneva), the debates centered on the defense of the one-unit theory in practice and its effect on areas traditionally regarded as high seas as well as the entire concept of an

[14] 5 Report of the Committee on the peaceful uses of the sea-bed and the ocean floor (SC. II/WG/Paper No. 4). The proposal is contained in Appendix D. As stated, *supra*, in footnote 8, the considerations that are incorporated in this proposal have already been analyzed, and an interpretative analysis will be provided.

[15] The problem of archipelagoes in the international law of the sea, pp. 556–567.

archipelagic State. The summary paragraphs containing the principal points of the Conference debate[16] are located in Appendix E, *infra.*

At the 1974 Law of the Sea Conference held in Caracas, the arguments became much more legally sophisticated and much more economically specific. The "archipelagic States" again attempted to justify their one-unit theory, but the fresh voice of the U.S.S.R. was added to the general interest position of the maritime States.[17]

The Soviet delegate's distress that the areas of high seas over which the archipelagic States wished to extend the sovereignty were larger than their total area of land reiterates the constantly repeated concern of the maritime States. So also, the Soviet view that any settlement over the conflict between the special interest and the general interest positions must continue to allow free transit through areas that have been traditionally regarded as open to international navigation. With respect to the proposals of the archipelagic States and the United Kingdom, it is apparent that the former proposal would allow all island chains to become archipelagic States whereas the later proposal would allow a State to declare itself to be an archipelagic State only if that State met the suggested criteria. In effect, the definitions emerging from each of the proposals seek to protect the special interests either of the archipelagic States or the general interests of the maritime nations.[18]

THE GEOGRAPHERS' PROPOSALS[19]

Having reviewed the two formal proposals submitted by the special-general interest groups, it is necessary to discuss two proposals, the first of which was published in 1972, prior to the United Nations Sea-bed Committee meeting (Geneva) held in 1973, and the second of which was published in 1973.[20] The Hodgson and Alexander proposal was concerned with setting forth specific limitations[21] to adjacency in order to prevent the application of a special

[16] 1 Report of the Committee on the peaceful uses of the sea-bed and the ocean floor, pp. 55–56. These debates were not officially recorded, *verbatum.* Instead, summaries of the arguments are set forth in vol. I of the six volume "Report of the Committee . . . ."

[17] United Nations Doc. A/CONF. 62/C.2/SR.37. See Appendix F.

[18] This dichotomy is discussed in more detail in the next two chapters.

[19] R. D. Hodgson and L. M. Alexander, "Towards an objective analysis of special circumstances . . .," Occasional paper no. 13, Law of the Sea Institute, Kingston, R. I., 1972. Robert D. Hodgson is the Director, Office of the Geographer, Bureau of Research and Intelligence, U.S. Department of State. Lewis M. Alexander is Director of Law of the Sea Institute, Rhode Island.

[20] Islands: normal and special circumstances, The Geographer, Bureau of Intelligence and Research (INR), U.S. Department of State, RGES-3, December 10, 1973, Washington D.C., 72 p.

[21] The only reason that is set forth for wanting a specific limitation is because The Geographers wish to avoid the possibility of all mid-ocean island groups from being treated with the same special status as archipelagic States. The implications of this limitation will be made fully evident in the discussion of the proposal in Chapter 7.

territorial regime concept from being applicable to all mid-ocean archipelagos.[22]

Regarding The Geographers' proposals, The Geographer, Bureau of Intelligence and Research,[23] suggests that modifications in their approach would be required if the proposals were to be applied to Indonesia and Philippines:

i) Adjacency. The proposal requires that, as a maximum, 40- to 48-nautical-mile closing lines be used as a measure of adjacency. These lines have since been applied to Indonesia, the Philippines, Fiji, the Galapagos, Tonga, and the Bahamas. The effects are minimal: In Indonesia, the islands of Sumatra, Borneo, Java, and the Celebes become a 'unit,' if a narrow connection may be declared unitized. The eastern areas remain detached and broken. The system works effectively for the remainder of the states, although the Philippines straight baselines would not enclose the Sulu Sea. *Pragmatically, neither the Philippines nor Indonesia is likely to accept the results of these lines unless other economic-resource zone limits would allocate the residual areas.* (Emphasis added.) Furthermore, these countries probably would want to hold that the waters within the baselines were internal waters, which would effectively close all Philippine and Indonesian straits except the Molucca-Ceram passage to Australia. The continuation of the route to East Asia would, nevertheless, be denied by the Philippine limits.

There is no evidence that The Geographers' conditions of adjacency had had any effect, either on the discussions at the United Nations Sea-bed Committee meetings in 1973 or at the Law of the Sea Conference in 1974.

The second proposal that was offered by The Geographer, Bureau of Research and Intelligence,[24] established a maximum permissible land-water ratio within the baselines.[25]

Neither of these proposals have gained acceptance, possibly because they do not resolve the resource allocation problem satisfactorily.[26]

The scattered references at Caracas revealed the same disagreement demonstrated at the earlier meetings of the U.N. Sea-bed Committee.[27] The special and general interest dichotomy continues. The deadlock persists.

[22] Towards an objective analysis of special circumstances . . ., pp. 45–46. This proposal is contained in Appendix G.

[23] Islands: normal and special circumstances, pp. 29–30.

[24] *Ibid.*, pp. 31–32.

[25] See Appendix H.

[26] The resource allocation problem is obviously fundamental to any proposed solution applying to mid-ocean archipelagos. It will be noted that this consideration is fundamental to the analysis set forth in Chapter VII, *infra.*

[27] U.N. Doc. A/CONF. 62/C.2/SR.37 (37th meeting, August 14, 1974).

CHAPTER VI

ON THE EMERGING DEFINITION OF AN ARCHIPELAGIC STATE

Throughout earlier chapters, the traditional terms and general concepts have been discussed with particular reference to the problems of coastal archipelagos, islands and delimitation of baselines. An analysis of the international conference preparatory materials and draft proposals and the writings of the publicists has been provided in order to highlight the difficulties confronting each legal writer and private scientific and scholarly organization in their attempts to (a) state the problem, (b) place the problem in a form capable of its resolution without being confined and limited to the traditional terms and general concepts that were never introduced or developed to meet the law of the sea problems of territorial waters of archipelagos, and (c) provide a solution to the dilemna.

Thus, having begun with an elementary analysis which provided a basic framework upon which to build (Chapter II), the next point of departure (Chapter III) was necessary to illustrate the distinction between coastal archipelagos, islands, and mid-ocean archipelagos. In order to accomplish this task, special problems of coastal archipelagos and groups of islands, in general, were introduced and analyzed so that the following chapter (Chapter IV) could bring together tall background materials, writings and thoughts regarding the entire subject as viewed by scholars. However, a peculiar failure was observed. Various publicists and organizations failed to distinguish between coastal archipelagos and mid-ocean archipelagos. They attempted to treat the problems (assuming that they recognized the existence of the problem) in the same manner, thereby precluding a viable result from being reached. This failure took place probably because the mid-ocean archipelagos were not independent States (being under colonial rule at the time). The metropolitan States were, in each instance, tranditionally large maritime nations that have constantly pressed for the greatest possible freedom of the use of the high seas. Therefore, the threat to international order, which is usually prerequisite to the development of the law in this area, was absent until the late 1950s.

It was not until 1973, at the United Nations Sea-bed Committee meeting (Geneva), that basically conflicting proposals were submitted, forcing the recognition that what was really at issue was the concept of the archipelagic State and its definition.

With these proposals in the foreground, it is necessary to trace briefly the development of the archipelagic-State concept in this chapter and thereafter to conclude this study with a chapter devoted to the framing of a resolution of the special-general interests dichotomy into a workable, concrete recommendation which hopefully may serve as a basis of discussion at the next law of the sea conference.

THE PHILIPPINES[1]

Since the Philippines was the first State to declare that they relied upon the archipelagic-State concept, let us first review the geographic location, size and extent of the Philippines:[2]

> The Republic of the Philippines consists of an archipelago of approximately 7,100 islands situated southeast of mainland Asia and separated from it by the South China Sea. The total land area is approximately 299,404 sq. km. (115,600 sq. mi.), 94% of which is contained within the 11 largest islands: Luzon (40,814 sq. mi.), Mindanao (36,906), Samar (5,050), Negros (4,905), Palawah (4,550), Panay (4,446), Mindoro (3,759), Leyte (2,785), Cebu (1,703), Bohol (1,492), and Masbate (1,262). Only 357 islands have areas that exceed 1 sq. mi. The Philippine archipelago lies approximately between 21°25′ and 4°23′ N (a distance of about 660 miles). It includes all the islands located therein except Palmas, which was ceded to the Netherlands (later, to Indonesia) in 1928. The archipelago trends NNW-SSE with Palawan Island and the Sulu Archipelago extending from the main group southwest toward Borneo; they are separated by the Balabac Strait and the Sibutu Passage, respectively. The Philippines' all-water boundaries include Bashi Channel to the north, the Pacific Ocean on the east, Celebes Sea to the South, and the South China Sea to the west.

THE PHILIPPINE DECLARATION

On December 12, 1955, the Ministry of Foreign Affairs of the Philippines delivered a note to the Secretary-General of the United Nations, which stated:[3]

> The position of the Philippine Government is that all waters around, between and connecting the different islands belonging to the Philippine Archipelago irrespective of their widths or dimensions, are necessary appurtenances of its land territory, forming an integral part of the national or inland waters, subject to the exclusive sovereignty of the

[1] The United States always treated each island (whether part of the Philippines or Hawaii, or any of its territories or possessions) as having its own belt of territorial waters. See discussion, *supra*, Chapter IV.

[2] Worldmark encyclopedia of the nations, 3rd ed., Ed., M. Y. Sachs, Asia and Australasia Ed.: Louis Barron, (Worldmark Press, Harper & Row, N.Y., 1967), vol. 4, p. 281.

[3] Laws and regulations on the regime of the territorial sea (U.N. legislative series, 1957), ST/LEG/SER.B/6, pp. 39040), as quoted and taken from 4 Whiteman Digest of international law, pp. 282–283.

Philippines. All other water areas embraced in the imaginary lines described in the Treaty of Paris of December 10, 1898 [Martens, *Nouveau Recueil general de traites*, 2eme serie, tome XXXII, p. 74/, the treaty concluded at Washington, D.C., between the United States and the United Kngdom [*ibid*, 3eme serie, tome XXVII, p. 58/, and the Convention of July 6, 1932 between the United States and Great Britain [*ibid.*, p. 66], as reproduced in Section 6 of Act No. 4003 and Article I of the Philippine Constitution, are considered as maritime territorial waters of the Philippines for purposes of protection of our fishing rights, conservation of our fishing resources, enforcement of revenue and anti-smuggling laws, defense and security, etc.

'It is the view of our Government that there is no rule of international law which defines or regulates the extent of the inland waters of a State.

The United States' position with regard to the declaration was that the lines stated in bilateral treaties between the United States and the United Kingdom and Spain merely delimited the area within which the land areas of the Philippines are located. Thus, the United States insisted that the lines outlined in the United States bilateral treaties are not to be taken as the outer boundary lines of the Philippine State.[4] Rather, the United States recognizes a three mile territorial sea limit for each island of the Philippines as it does for each island of the Hawaiian chain.[5]

THE PHILIPPINE DECLARATION IN PRACTICE

Six years after the delivery of its note to the Secretary-General of the United Nations, the Philippines approved Republic Act No. 3046[6] whereby all waters within the baselines were considered "internal." Instantly, on the same day, the United States addressed a Note of Protest to the Philippine government, declaring, in part, that:

. . . the United States Government could not regard claims based on the present legislation as binding upon it or its nationals.[7]

Pursuant to the Act, the Philippines drew a series of 80 straight baselines around the external group of islands. The length of the baseline system is 8,174.8974 nautical miles.[8] The average length of a segment is 102.185 nautical miles. The longest baseline segment is 140.05 nautical miles. The

[4] The treaty article, together with Professor Sorenson's comments thereon, are discussed, *supra*, Chapter IV. The United States' position with regard to the declaration is set forth in 4 Whiteman digest of international law, pp. 283–284. See Appendix H-1.

[5] See discussion, *supra*, Chapter IV.

[6] This Act is formerly referred to as: An act to define the baselines of the territorial sea of the Philippines (as taken from International boundary study, Series A, Limits in the seas, No. 33, pp. 1–7, Straight baselines: The Philippines, Office of the Geographer, Dept. of State, Bureau of Intelligence and Research, 1973).

[7] Embassy note no. 836, *ibid.*, p. 8.

[8] All of the figures contained herein are extracted from the International boundary study, p. 148.

baseline system, in effect, closes the international passages—Surigao Sibutu Passage, Balabac Strait and Mindoro Strait—as well as the more "internal" passages through the Philippine islands. The Indonesian island of Pulau Miangas, in the extreme southeast, is contained within the Philippine territorial sea and the Indonesian straight baselines. The straight baseline system connects the outermost points of the islands. The approximate land area of the system is 115,600 square (statute) miles or 87,278 square nautical miles. The area contained within the straight baselines measures 328,345 square miles or 247,845 square nautical miles. *The enclosure system therefore increases the territory of the Philippines approximately 2.8 fold.* The resulting land (115,600 square miles) to water (328,345–115,600 equals 212,745 square miles) ratio is approximately 1:1,841. The use of the treaty limits as the territorial sea boundary would raise the total Philippine area to 702,460 square miles or 530,239 square nautical miles *thereby increasing by more than 2.14 the territory within the baselines.*[9] The ratio of land and internal waters to territorial sea (374,115 square miles) is 1,139 while the land to territorial sea ratio is 1:3,236. The ratio of land to territorial and internal waters is approximately 1:5,065. The full implications of the proportion of total land to total sea areas will be examined in connection with the proposal in the final Chapter VII.

INDONESIA

The second reliance upon the concept of an archipelagic State is the even more complicated and difficult case of Indonesia. The geographical extent and resulting complications follow from a review of its location and size:[10]

The Republic of Indonesia consists of six large islands and more than 3,000 small islands forming an archipelago between Asia and Australia and reaching from 95° to 140° E (about 3,275 miles) and from 6°N to 11°S (about 1,373 miles). The principal island groups are the Greater Sunda Islands comprising Java and Madura (51,000 sq. mi.), Sumatra (164,000 sq. mi.), Borneo (72% of which, or 208,000 sq. mi., belongs to Indonesia and is known as Kalimantan), Sulawesi (formerly called Celebes, 73,000 sq. mi.) and adjoining smaller islands; the Lesser Sunda (Nusa Tenġgara) Islands; the Maluku Islands (moluccas); and New Guinea (the western portion—159,375 sq. mi.—belongs to Indonesia and is known as West Irian or Irian Barat).

Northern and Northwestern Borneo consists of Sabah and Sarawak (Malaysia and the British protectorate of Brunei. The eastern half of Timor, one of the Lesser Sunda group, is controlled by Portugal.) The Indonesia land areas is 1,904,345 sq. km. (735,267 sq. mi.). Indonesia is bounded by the South China Sea on the north, the Pacific Ocean on the north and east, and the Indian Ocean on the south and west.

[9] It will be recalled that one of the main arguments presented by the Russian delegation at the 1974 Law of the Sea Conference (Caracas) concerned the vast areas of high seas that would fall within the jurisdictional authorities of the archipelagic States if the formal proposal of these States were followed. See the delegate's comments, *supra*, Chapter V.

[10] 4 Worldmark encyclopedia, p. 103.

THE INDONESIAN DECLARATION

On December 14, 1957, the Government of Indonesia issued an Announcement on the territorial waters of the Republic of Indonesia. It was stated, in part, in the Announcement that:[11]

> Historically, the Indonesian archipelago has been an entity since time immemorial.
>
> In view of territorial entirety and of preserving the wealth of the Indonesian state, it is deemed necessary to consider all waters between the islands an entire entity.
>
> . . .
>
> On the ground of the above considerations, the Government states that all waters around, between and connecting, the islands or parts of islands belonging to the Indonesian archipelago irrespective of their width or dimension are natural appurtenances of its land territory and therefore an integral part of the inland or national waters subject to the absolute sovereignty of Indonesia. *The peaceful passage of foreign vessels through these waters is guaranteed as long and insofar as it is not contrary to the sovereignty of the Indonesian state or harmful to her security.* (Emphasis added.) The delimitation of the territorial sea, with a width of 12 nautical miles, shall be measured from straight base lines connecting the outermost points of the islands of the Republic of Indonesia.

This declaration also led to protests by the United States and other nations. The United States and Australia promptly delivered notes of protest to the Indonesian foreign office on December 31, 1957 and January 15, 1958, respectively.[12] In addition, the Japanese Vice Minister for Foreign Affairs (Katsumi Ohno) protested the declaration in a communication on January 13, 1958.[13]

Despite the numerous protests, the declaration was enacted into law by Indonesia on February 18, 1960.[14]

The historic position of the Dutch government throughout the Netherlands Indies period was published in the 1939 enactment: Territorial sea and maritime districts ordinances.[15] The ordinance provided, in part, that for

[11] 4 Whiteman digest of international law 284 (with no reference to an original publication). With reference to the above announcement, Mr. Syatauw, in his book (Some newly established Asian States and the development of international law, The Hague: Martinus Nijhoff, 1961) states (in his footnote 190 at p. 173 of his book) that the translation of this announcement was published in the Indonesian law journal, Hakum, vol. 1958, no. 5–6, Annex 1 and also was printed in an Indonesian newspaper article (Keng Po, 14 December 1957).

[12] 4 Whiteman digest of international law, pp. 284–285. See Appendix H-2.

[13] Japanese Vice Minister for Foreign Affairs Katsumi Ohno to the Indonesian Consul General at Tokyo, M. Iskandar Ishaq, January 13, 1958, The Japanese annual of international law, No. 2 (The Japan Branch of the International Law Association, 1958), pp. 219–220 (as taken from 4 Whiteman digest of international law 285). See Appendix H-3.

[14] The legislation is known as Act No. 4 and it is published, in English, in United Nations Doc. A/CONF. 19/5/Add. 1 (1960), pp. 3–4.

[15] Staatsblad van Nederlands Indie (Official gazette of the Netherlands Indies) 1939, no. 442, translated by the Secretariat of the United Nations and printed in Laws and regulations of the regime of the territorial sea, U.N. Leg. Ser. 193–201 (ST/LEG/SER. B/6) (1957), as taken from Mr. Syatauw's article, Indonesia and the law of the sea, *op. cit.*, p. 170.

islands, the three-mile limit was to be measured from straight lines:

> . . . connecting the outermost points of the low water marks of the islands on the outer edge of the group, at the point where distance between these points is not more than six miles.[16]

In the steps leading to Indonesia's independence (which occurred on December 29, 1949), Article 8 of the Agreement on transitional measures[17] was adopted by the constitution of the United States of Indonesia (Article 192) and since 1950, it has become Article 142 of the provisional constitution of the Republic of Indonesia.[18] According to Mr. Syatauw, Indonesia's position is that the maritime legislation in force during the Dutch colonial period is incompatible with the transfer of sovereignty and therefore was effectively revoked by subsequent legislation: namely, the Indonesian declaration of December 13, 1957.[19]

THE INDONESIAN DECLARATION IN PRACTICE

Currently, the Indonesian straight baseline system extends for 8,167.6 nautical miles. The system encloses approximately 666,000 square nautical miles of internal waters including the important straits of Sunda, Sumba, Lombok, Ombai, Molucca and Macassar as well as numerous internal passages within the Indonesian archipelago. The system contains 196 individual segments with an average length of 41.67 nautical miles.[20] Because of the fact that the Indonesian territorial sea claim extends seaward for 12 nautical miles from the straight baselines, *an additional 98,000 square nautical miles of water falls under Indonesian sovereignty.* Again, the full implications of the proportion of total land to total sea areas will be examined in connection with the proposal in the final Chapter VII, *infra.*

With the advent of the end of the colonial period, together with independence and the unilateral declarations accompanying this transition (due to the need for extensive fishing and mineral rights) and the various protests of governments, there emerged an obvious conflict between the special and general interest groups. In order for the one-unit theorists the enlarge the resource intake of the "archipelagic States," areas of "high seas" (if discussing the matter in conventional terms) would have to be eliminated.

[16] *Ibid.*, Article 1, paragraph 1B (Mr. Syatauw's article, p. 171).

[17] As taken from Mr. Syatauw's article, *op. cit.*, p. 172.

[18] The code books, statutes and ordinances including the provisional constitution of the Republic of Indonesia, 17, 33, 67 and 95 (1956) (as taken from Mr. Syatauw's article, *op. cit.*, p. 111).

[19] *Ibid.*, pp. 172–173.

[20] All of the figures contained herein are extracted from: International boundary study, Series A, Limits in the seas, Straight baselines, Indonesia, Bureau of Intelligence and Research, Office of the Geographer, U.S. Department of State, No. 35, July 20, 1971.

These diametrically opposed general and special interest groups reached their respective polarized positions and set forth joint declarations and protests concerning archipelagic States without even having the "benefit" of, or defining the term, "archipelagic State." It was not until the 1973 Geneva United Nations Sea-bed Committee meeting that definitions of the term were set forth.[21] The definitions served to further alienate the groups because it is obvious that their definitions of an archipelagic State were based upon their respective solutions to the resource allocation/international navigation problems.[22]

AN ARCHIPELAGIC-STATE DEFINED

Against this background, it appears that, for purposes of discussion, an archipelagic State may be defined as a group of three or more islands that are so united by geographical, economic, political and historical ties that the islands or portions thereof (not the seas that flow between them) are considered as an entity. This definition precludes States such as Japan, Australia and the United Kingdom because these countries have not historically been treated as archipelagos but rather as mainland-type States.[23] In addition, the definition precludes the argument against the one-unit theory that if archipelagic States enclose areas of high seas, the total square miles of high-seas areas would be more than the total square miles of island space.

Lastly, the proposed recommendation in the final chapter will demonstrate that this definition can be applied and still satisfy the special and general interest groups thereby erasing the threat posed to international order. Also, the recommendation could be applicable to mid-ocean archipelagos that are not archipelagic States.

Recognizing the fact that both archipelagic States and non-archipelagic States are using the term, "archipelagic State," *a definition of the term has not, and still does not, solve the problem of delimitation that is presented in this study.* The problem exists; the dilemma lingers on.

[21] The definition proposed by Indonesia, Philippines, Fiji and Mauritius is set forth, *supra*, Chapter V, the United Kingdom definition is given, *supra*, Chapter V.

[22] For instance, the one-unit theorists were not going to limit the length of baselines because this would eliminate the consideration of the archipelago as one unit thereby limiting the resources available to them. The interests of each group were placed into the framework of a definition rather than attempting to resolve each interest to the satisfaction of both groups.

[23] As will be discussed in the proposal given, *infra*, Chapter VII, countries with one large island and a few smaller fringe islands that are located in close proximity to the main island (e.g., Australia and the United Kingdom) would not benefit from being treated as one unit because the few fringe islands would expand the baseline delimitation seawards for a few miles only.

CHAPTER VII

A PROPOSED RECOMMENDATION FOR DETERMINING THE TERRITORIAL WATERS OF ARCHIPELAGOS (WHETHER CONSTITUTING A SINGLE STATE OR PORTION OF A STATE)

THE CLASSIC PROBLEM OF THE RESOLUTION OF CONFLICTING INTERESTS IN THE LAW OF THE SEA: SPECIAL INTERESTS V. GENERAL INTERESTS

Throughout the latter part of this book, it has been observed that the "special interests" of the archipelagic States constitute sufficient reason for the adoption of special law of the sea rules. A review of the conventional international law that is applicable to coastal States and coastal archipelagos would suggest that these special interests are: customs, fiscal policy, immigration, sanitation, communications (both internal and external), illegal entry of aliens, pollution control and natural resources (e.g., fishing and minerals).[1]

A similar review would include, under the "general interests" of the maritime nations, the four freedoms in Article 2, Convention on the High Seas.[2] To these rights, it is believed that this book has established that the more important editions to the "*inter alia*" list of Article 2 are resource allocation (e.g., fishing and mineral) and baseline delimitation formulae.

LIMITATIONS ON THE USE OF PRECEDENT

Legal writers become bogged down when attempting to resolve the delimitation problem presented herein within the confines of traditional conventional terms: for example, internal waters, territorial waters (sea), contiguous zone, continental shelf, baselines, innocent passage and so forth. It has been demonstrated

[1] It is perhaps significant that the term "security" was deliberately eliminated from the four areas enumerated as falling within the contiguous zone (customs, fiscal policy, immigration and sanitation):
"(4) The Commission did not recognize special security rights in the contiguous zone. It considered that the extreme vagueness of the term 'security' would open the way for abuses and that the granting of such rights was not necessary. The enforcement of customs and sanitary regulations will be sufficient in most cases to safeguard the security of the State . . . ." Report of the International Law Commission covering the work of its eighth session, 23 April–4 July 1956, U.N. Gen. Ass. off. rec. 11th Sess., Supp. No. 9 (A/3159), p. 39; III U.N. Conf. on the Law of the Sea, First Committee (territorial sea and contiguous zone) commentary to Article 66 (as taken from 4 Whiteman digest of international law, pp. 483–485). Doc. A/3159, pp. 39–40; II Yearbook of the International Law Commission, 1956, pp. 253, 294–295.

[2] Article 2 is discussed, *supra*, Chapter II.

that none of the international law of the sea conferences were able to resolve the delimitation problem in the context of the special interest/general interest conflict. In addition, the various traditional and conventional terms were applied in the customary international law and in the discussions and international treaties at the principal international conferences on the law of the sea for application to large territorial mainlands and were extended, with some success, to offshore islands and coastal archipelagos, but were never envisioned to apply either to archipelagic States or mid-ocean archipelagos.[3]

Having in mind all of these difficulties, and in response to the challenge that they provide, an effort will now be made to formulate a solution for the delimitation problems of mid-ocean archipelagos. It is believed that the study to this point has established that no single formula will resolve the delimitation problems.

The first stage of analysis for the shape of a solution is a recognition that the special interests of the archipelagic States may be usefully divided into two groups: (*a*) natural resources—e.g., fishing and minerals; (*b*) non-natural resources—customs, fiscal policy, immigration, sanitation, communications (both internal and external), illegal entry of aliens and pollution control.

This distinction can, of course, only be made in the application of a formula that will be drawn out of the basic geographical considerations of the mid-ocean archipelago. The geographical reality is that each archipelagic state is composed of islands that are situated at unequal distances from each other. There are at least three possibilities:

(1) The islands are scattered, at random, over a radius of more than twice the breadth of the territorial sea and are not grouped together in any particular pattern. In this situation, there occurs wide areas of high seas between the islands:

[3] Despite all of the discussions at the 1958 Geneva Law of the Sea Conference, there was a dismal failure in connection with resolving the problems regarding the questions of the breadth of

(2) The islands are not scattered over a large distance. Instead, they are grouped together, at random, with smaller areas of high seas flowing between the islands:

(3) There is one large mainland-type island with a few islands located within a close proximity both to the large island and to the other fringe islands. In this situation, the total square miles of high seas flowing between all of the islands is less than the total square miles of island mass:[4]

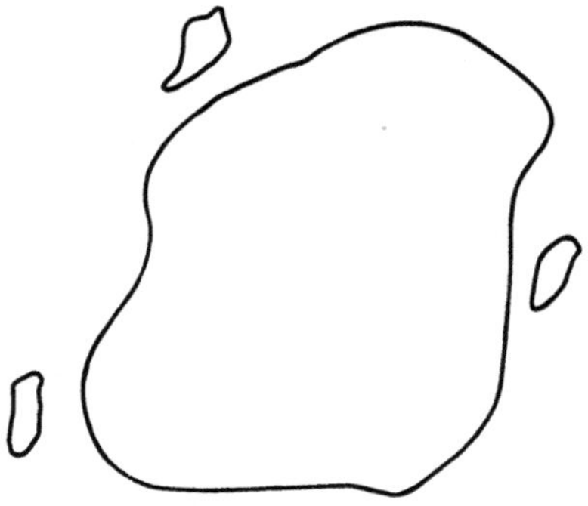

the territorial sea and fishery limits. Recognizing the fact that these problems would have to be solved, the Conference adopted a resolution requesting the General Assembly of the United Nations to study the advisability of convening a second international conference. The General Assembly resolved to ask the Secretary-General to convoke a second conference in March or April, 1960 "... for the purpose of considering further the questions of the breadth of the territorial sea and fishery limits" (Resolution VIII, adopted April 27, 1958, Doc. A/CONF. 13/L.56; II U.N. Conf. on the Law of the Sea, Plenary Meetings (A/CONF. 13/38), p. 145; Resolution 1307 (XIII), was adopted by the General Assembly on December 10, 1958, by a vote of 71 in favor, 0 opposed, and 6 abstentions), taken from 4 Whiteman digest of international law, p. 119.

However, the 1960 Conference again ended in dismal failure leaving both questions unresolved.

[4] However, after conferring with Mr. Hodgson, The Geographer, U.S. Department of State, it was not possible to give any examples of archipelagic states that fit into this geographical situation. The term "archipelagic State", as defined by the proposals discussed in Chapter V and VI, precludes States such as Japan, United Kingdom, Australia from treating themselves as archipelagic States because they have not, historically, viewed their State as falling within this category nor have they been treated as such. This lack of historical treatment could be attributed to the fact that these States are composed of one or more large islands with only a few fringe islands of much smaller size. Nevertheless, there is no reason why the proposal submitted in this chapter could not be applicable to all mid-ocean archipelagos.

PROPOSED SOLUTION

For all three situations, it is submitted that an archipelagic State should be permitted to employ a straight baseline *method* in order to enclose all of the islands and the waters lying between and around said islands. The resulting line would not be a baseline for these purposes but would serve as an *indicator* only.[5] As will be seen later, the *indicator* would be utilized in the delimitation of the fishing and mineral rights of the archipelagic State. As was observed earlier, current unilateral practices of archipelagic States use the one-unit concept wherein waters located to the interior of the baseline are treated as "internal," and waters to the exterior of the baseline, and outward to a specified distance, are treated as "territorial." Thus, archipelagic States are attempting to apply traditional terms to unconventional areas thereby claiming competence to prescribe and enforce their laws over vast "high-seas" areas.

In order to illustrate the use of the *indicator*, it is necessary to examine, specifically, its applicability to natural resource allocation (e.g., fishing and mineral).

FISHING RIGHTS

With reference to fishing rights, the *indicator* would be used for all mid-ocean archipelagos, whether they consist of (1) islands that are scattered, at random, over a radius of more than twice the breadth of the territorial sea and are not grouped together in any particular pattern, (2) islands that are not scattered over a large distance but are grouped together, at random, with smaller areas of high seas flowing between the islands, or (3), one large mainland-type island with a few islands located within a close proximity both to the large island and to the other smaller islands. The use of the *indicator* is illustrated on p. 70.

Let us take another look at the illustration and assuming that the standard territorial sea (or, alternatively, economic zone area) claimed by all nations is 12 miles (or, alternatively, 200 miles economic zone), the coastal State would have exclusive fishing rights within the 12-mile limit and would share high-seas areas freely with other nations. However, islands that are scattered, at random, over twice the breadth of the territorial sea and are not grouped together in any particular pattern have vast areas of high seas falling within the *indicator*. The archipelagic State is gaining extra fishing rights because of the physical location of the islands.

Therefore, in order that the archipelagic State does not gain undue fishing advantages at the expense of hitherto high-seas-fishing users because of the

[5] With the proposed method, the *indicator* would be identical to the baseline delimitation as determined by the existing customary and conventional law.

geographical layout of its islands, it should be permitted to use all areas within the *indicator* to the exclusion of other States. However, the total square miles of the area within the *indicator*, less the land area, should be calculated. This total should be deducted from the total area of the territorial sea band outside the *indicator*. Thus, an archipelagic State could conceivably have only a very limited fishing area band outside the *indicator*. In no case, however, would the archipelagic State fishing area be less than the total area within the *indicator*.

- - - - - - - = "Indicator"

———————— = "Outer perimeter of territorial sea"

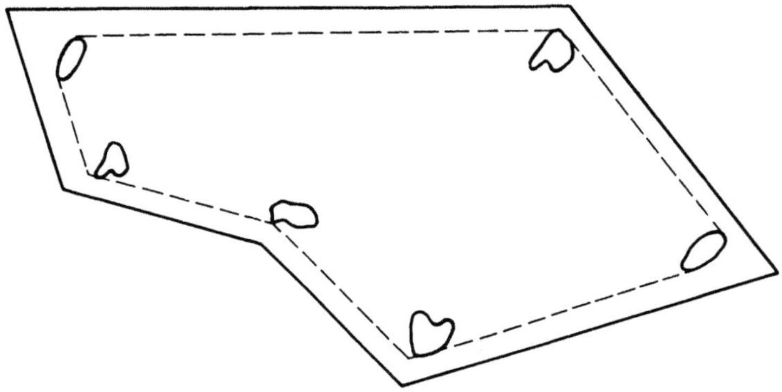

Use of the indicator

Mineral rights

With reference to mineral rights, the *indicator* is based on a hypothetical composite geological limitation of the continental shelf (or, alternatively, an economic zone that either replaces or supplements the use of the continental shelf). This would be true whether the mid-ocean archipelagos consist of (1) islands that are scattered, at random, over a radius of more than twice the breadth of the territorial sea and are not grouped together in any particular pattern, (2) islands that are not scattered over a large distance but are grouped together, at random, with smaller areas of high seas flowing between the islands, or (3) one large mainland-type island with a few islands located within a close proximity to the other smaller islands. The use of the *indicator* is illustrated in the composite sketch on page 71.[6] In this illustration, the determina-

[6] A composite sketch is utilized because the geological formation of the continental shelf varies from zero to more than 800 miles around each continent. ". . . The entire submerged area between the islands of Sumatra, Java and Borneo is covered by water less than 300 feet deep . . . ." See discussion contained, *supra*, Chapter II, and extensively covered in Zdenek J. Slouka's book (International custom and the continental shelf, p. 6)

tion of continental shelf is subject to legal criteria[7] but this would not prevent the use of the same *indicator* formula.

The total number of square miles of continental shelf area within the *indicator* less the total miles of non-continental shelf area within the *indicator* would be deducted from the total number of square miles of continental shelf area located outside of the *indicator*. In contrast to the fishing area where the reductions would reduce the amount of the territorial sea band (e.g., from 12 to 11 miles or 12 to one mile, but in no case more than the territorial sea band),[8] there would not be a reduction of a territorial sea as in the fishing example, but a

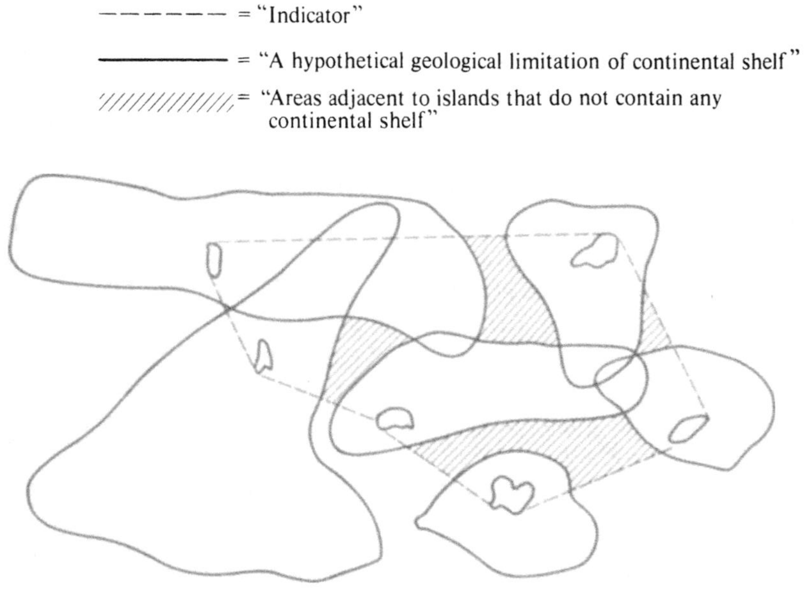

A composite sketch concerning mineral rights and the indicator

possible giving up of excess continental shelf area outside of the *indicator* in order to bring the archipelagic State into parity with other nations (or for the common heritage of mankind). In no case, however, would the archipelagic State receive less continental shelf than the total amount within the *indicator*. The determination, in a particular conceivable instance, of what particular continental shelf areas outside of the *indicator* would be chosen to make up the

[7] The legal criteria is discussed in Chapter II.

[8] It so happens that all of the archipelagic states have 12-mile territorial sea limits and the illustrations in the text, accordingly, reflect that fact. If the territorial sea limits of the archipelagic states were to be established at say 50 miles, the relative illustrations, as in the 12-mile case, could be 49 or one mile, respectively; if the territorial sea limits of the archipelagic states were to be established at say 200 miles, the relative illustrations, as in the 12 mile case, could be 199 or one mile, respectively.

necessary total of excess continental shelf area, would be a question of providing the appropriate international treaty provisions and probably the appropriate machinery within which the archipelagic State would obtain acceptance of its adjustment of its continental shelf claims. These problems may arise, but the application of the *indicator* formula to mineral rights is highly possible and desirable.

It is obvious from reading the Third United Nations Conference on the Law of the Sea informal single negotiating text and Text on settlement of disputes (reproduced by Office of Law of the Sea Negotiations, Department of State, Washington, D.C., May 9, 1975) that the current law of the sea convention is moving towards the creation of a 200-mile economic zone. This zone will be utilized to determine fishing rights and will be substituted for, or supplement, the continental shelf provisions in order to determine mineral rights. This is a strong possibility but the attitude of the States with vast continental shelves, in excess of 200 miles, will have to be taken into account. Their consent to this economic zone will be needed.

The usefulness of the proposed *indicator* formula can be tested by reviewing the boundary studies of the two principal archipelagic States (Indonesia and the Philippines) that were prepared by The Geographer, United States Department of State.[9] A quick glance at the total miles in these two studies indicate that these two countries consist of islands that are scattered, at random, over a radius of more than twice the breadth of the territorial sea and are not grouped together in any particular patters. In both cases, it is clear that they would not receive any additional exclusive fishing rights. So also, in the case of Mauritius[10] and Fiji.[11]

In addition to archipelagic States, certain States have applied the one-unit

[9] The total miles are set forth, *supra*, Chapter VI. These two studies are the only boundary analyses that were prepared by The Geographer that give the complete, comparative total square miles inside the *indicator* (baselines) and outside the *indicator* seaward to a distance of 12 miles, the same being the total square miles of the breadth or perimeter of the territorial sea. The Geographer advises that other boundary studies have been prepared but are not for general publication, as yet.

[10] "The State of Mauritius comprises the following territories:

a) the principal island of Mauritius and its adjacent islets;
b) Rodrigues Island, a coralline near-atoll situated approximately 300 nautical miles eastward from Mauritius;
c) The Cargados Carajos Shoals, a true atoll situated approximately 220 nautical miles north-north-east of Mauritius; and
d) the Agalega Islands, two narrow, linearly-aligned islands situated nearly 650 nautical miles north of Mauritius."

International boundary study, Series A, Limits in the seas, Straight baselines, Mauritius, U.S. Dept of State, No. 41, March 7, 1972, p. 5.

[11] Fiji comprises more than 300 islands (106 of them inhabited), scattered over 95,000 square miles of sea, between 15° and 22°S. and 177°W. and 175°E. Total area is 7,055 sq. miles. Two main islands, Viti Levu and Vanua Levu, comprise over 85% of the land area. Worldmark encyclopedia of the nations, 3rd ed., Ed: M. Y. Sachs, Asia and Australasia Ed.: Louis Barron, Worldmask Press, Harper & Row, N.Y. (1967), vol. 4, p. 353.

concept to their mid-ocean archipelagos.[12] For purposes of illustration, the Galapagos Islands (i.e., Colon archipelago) and the Faeroe Islands[13] will serve, possibly, to illustrate either a situation where the islands are scattered, at random, over a radius of more than twice the breadth of the territorial sea and are not grouped together in any particular pattern or, possibly, illustrate a situation where the islands are not scattered over a large distance but are grouped together, at random, with smaller areas of high seas flowing between the islands.[14] The States of Indonesia, Philippines, Mauritius and Fiji serve to demonstrate an example of mid-ocean islands that are scattered, at random, over a radius of more than twice the breadth of the territorial sea and are not grouped together in any particular pattern. These States would not receive any exclusive fishing areas seaward of the *indicator* because the total square miles of high seas within the *indicator* is so excessively large. Malta can serve as an illustration of islands that are not scattered over a large distance but are grouped together, at random, with smaller areas of high seas flowing between the islands where the land to water ratio is probably 1:1 thereby permitting a full perimeter of territorial sea around the indicator.[15]

Having demonstrated the application of the *indicator formula* to resource uses of the seas, let us now turn to a discussion of the second part of the

[12] A discussion of the legislative and executive decrees, declarations and the practice of states is located, *supra*, Chapter IV.

[13] These islands are located in the Atlantic Ocean, due north of Scotland, between 61°26′ and 62°24′N. and 6°15′ and 7°41′W. The 19 islands, 18 of which are inhabited, cover an area of 1,399 sq. km. (540 sq. mi.). Among the larger islands are Stromo (374 sq. km.), Ostero (286 sq. km.), Vaago (178 sq. km.), Sydero (153 sq. km.), and Sando (114 sq. km.). 5 Worldmark encyclopedia, p. 73.

Denmark decreed, on April 24, 1963, straight baselines to encircle the Faeroe Islands. The decree came into effect on March 12, 1964 and stated, in part:

"*Section 1.* The boundary within which only Faeroese and other Danish nationals shall be authorized to engage in fishing, shall be a line 12 nautical miles from the baselines described in par. 2, drawn as shown on the map adjoined as an annex to the present Decree. . . ." International boundary study, Series A, Limits in the seas: Straight baselines, Faeroes, No. 13, issued March 12, 1970, p. 2.

The decree created thirteen straight baseline segments which surrounded the archipelago. The straight baselines enclosed off the east and west shores, a considerable amount of water area. The thirteen straight baseline segments have a total length of 163.0 nautical miles. They vary from .1 to 60.8 nautical miles in length with an average of 12.53 nautical miles. Two of the segments (44.0 and 60.8 nautical miles) exceed 24 nautical miles; five measure 1 mile or less in length. The ratio of water to land enclosed by the Faeroese straight baselines is less than 2:1.

[14] The Faeroe Islands could conceivably fall within either situation because of the small ratio of water to land that is enclosed by the straight baselines (less than 2:1). However these islands do not constitute an archipelagic state. Instead, they could serve to illustrate the application of the *indicator formula* to states that possess mid-ocean archipelagos.

[15] Malta is located in the central Mediterranean Sea, 58 miles south of Sicily and 180 miles from the nearest point of the North African mainland. It includes three islands: Malta (17 miles long and 9 miles wide); Gozo (9 miles long and 4.5 miles wide), to the northwest; Comino, between them; and two small uninhabited islands, Cominotto and Filfla. Its total area is 121.8 sq. miles (Malta, 94.9 sq. mi.; Gozo, 25.9 sq. mi.; and Comino, 1 sq. mi.). 5 Worldmark encyclopedia, p. 189.

proposed solution where the *indicator formula* does not lend itself to application; namely, the non-resource uses of the seas, whether high seas, contiguous zone, territorial waters (sea) or internal waters.

Non-Resource Uses of the Sea: Customs, Fiscal Policy, Immigration, Sanitation, Communications (internal and external) and Pollution Control

Here, as in the case of the resource allocation problem, the basic need is to achieve an acceptable compromise between the presently polarized general and special interest groups. This list of the principal non-resource uses is generally dealt with in the traditional terms of the conventional law by providing for their coverage within certain jurisdictional catègories such as internal waters, territorial seas and contiguous zone concepts. The application of the traditional terms to mid-ocean archipelagos raises great difficulties.

The following procedure is suggested:

(1) A list of the non-resource interests be drawn based upon those uses provided to all States under conventional law.

(2) A list of distances from the baselines around each island necessary to protect these non-resource uses shall be prepared.

(3) The list of non-resource uses and the appropriate distances shall be reasonable and proper under all the circumstances.

(4) The two lists shall be determined in the first instance by the archipelagic States; and, in the second instance, agreed to by the other lawmaking Conference States.

Thus, both the special interest group and the general interest group are protected. The archipelagic States neither lose their competence to prescribe or enforce the exercise of the listed uses within the agreed distances nor gain large masses of ocean that are currently considered high seas. The main difficulty with this procedure is that it would probably be difficult and time consuming for Conference States to agree on the uses and respective distances. The drafting problems would be substantial but not insurmountable.

Possible alternative procedures can be envisioned. An alternative procedure is to agree to a list of non-resource uses but to provide a uniform distance that would be common to an enjoyment of all the listed uses.

A third alternative procedure may be an adoption of the Alexander-Hodgson proposal,[16] which, it will be recalled, provided for the breaking up of islands in a mid-ocean archipelago into groups of islands, each of which is located no more than forty nautical miles from any other group. Each group of islands would have its indicator and perimeter for natural and non-natural resources. The consequence in this formula, of course, would be to greatly increase the high-seas areas within the mid-ocean archipelagos.

A final stage in the testing of the effectiveness of the *indicator formula* would

[16] This proposal is set forth, *supra*, Chapter V.

be to examine examples of the two extreme situations. In the one case, the present United States-administered Trust Territory of Micronesia, now moving towards independence, is an example of a very large number (2,141) of very small islands, spread over a very large area (some 3 million square miles) in the western Pacific Ocean.[17]

Micronesia, Second Special Session, 1972,[18] and completed at the Fifth Congress of Micronesia, First Regular Session, 1973, proceeded to define the terms over the Micronesian claim[19] and not surprisingly accepted the one-unit theory asserted by Indonesia and the Philippines.[20] Even though the United States is the sponsor of Micronesian independence, it will oppose this claim. The other maritime States may also be expected to object.[21]

It is believed that this predictable international conflict could be avoided if an *indicator* formula were utilized, not for the whole of the land and sea territory of Micronesia, but on the basis of each of the six administrative districts of Micronesia.[22] These administrative districts, which have been utilized since July 1, 1947 (the islands formally became a United Nations trust territory under United States administration) for the administration of the Trusteeship, appeàr to be based on the total area of the separate island chains (Caroline, Marshall and Mariana).[23] With such modification as to rely upon island groupings, there is no reason to believe that the *indicator formula* proposal would not be fundamentally efficient.

Turning to the other extreme of one large mainland-type island with a few islands located within a close proximity both to the large island and to the other smaller islands,[24] the application of the *indicator formula* is entirely possible but not particularly appropriate. The result of applying the formula would add very little existing high seas area to the present land-sea total area. This is true because most of these States contain one large or several island masses with a

[17] See Appendix I.

[18] Public law 4C-92.

[19] Senate joint resolution No. 40, S.D. 1 Fifth Congress of Micronesia.

[20] Law of the sea: The preliminary Micronesian position prepared by Joint Committee on the Law of the Sea, Fifth Congress of Micronesia, Saipan, Mariana Islands, May 14, 1973.

[21] The United States position regarding the unilateral declaration of Indonesia and the Philippines has been discussed throughout this study. For example, see the formal protests of the United States (and other nations), *supra*, Chapter VI.

[22] The six districts are set forth in Appendix I.

[23] The total area of the three separate island chains is set forth in Appendix I. Authority for all of the trust territory is vested in a high commissioner, appointed by the United States President and under the immediate authority of the Secretary of the Interior. The high commissioner appoints a district commissioner to each of the six districts. 5 Worldmark encyclopedia, p. 361.

[24] For example, the traditional island states, such as Japan, the United Kingdom, Australia and Ireland, could request receiving the same treatment as the archipelagic states, as defined. The suggested definition precludes such states from archipelagic-state-type treatment. See definition located, *supra*, Chapter VI.

few closely adjoining islands.[25] Ireland will be used for the purpose of illustration:[26]

An island in the eastern part of the North Atlantic on the continental shelf of Europe, Ireland is bounded on the northeast by the North Channel, which separates it from Scotland, on the east and southeast by the Irish Sea and St. George's Channel, which separate it from England and Wales. To the west, from north to south, the coast is washed by the Atlantic Ocean, which separates Ireland from North America by more than 2,000 miles. Situated between 51°30′ and 55°30′ N. and 5°30′ and 10°30′ W., Ireland covers an area of 32,595 sq. mi., of which 27,136 sq. mi. are in the republic, the remainder in Northern Ireland, a part of the UK. The island's greatest length, measured from NNE to SSW, is 302 miles; from east to west, 171 miles.

Currently, Ireland employs straight baselines as a result of Statutory Instrument No. 173, effective January 1, 1960, said statute supplementing the Irish Maritime Jurisdiction Act, 1959, which came into effect on October 1, 1959.[27] The boundary study prepared by the United States Department of State in connection with these straight baselines, asserts that:[28]

The Irish Government has applied the straight baseline principle in a unique manner. Six straight baselines alternate with seven normal baselines utilizing the low water line of the mainland or of adjacent islands. The eastern coast, on the Irish Sea, which is generally only locally indented and which lacks offshore islands, has not been supplemented by straight baselines. In the north, the coast between the boundary fjord (Lough Foyle) and Malin Head, a point on Ireland's North Point, forms the baseline. To the west and south, however, a series of baselines stretch to the southeast cape of Ireland. The straight baselines have replaced the low water line for more than 90% of the coast.

Ireland would hardly gain any advantage by using the *indicator formula* proposal suggested herein.

The application of the proposal has been examined in the principal specific archipelagic situations of Indonesia, the Philippines, Mauritius, Fiji, the Galapagos and Faeroe Islands and Malta,[29] and including the two extreme

[25] It is interesting to observe that these states could treat the smaller islands as coastal archipelagos to achieve approximately the same results as the application of the *indicator formula*, assuming there is no drastic change from the present *general* 12-mile territorial sea limit.

[26] 5 Worldmark encyclopedia, p. 157.

The Republic of Iceland is another example. It is the westernmost country of Europe, being an island in the North Atlantic Ocean just below the Arctic Circle and a little over 200 miles east of Greenland:

"It extends from 13°30′ to 24°32′W. (about 300 miles) and from 63°24′ to 66°32′N. (about 190 miles), and has an area of about 103,000 sq. km. (39,758 sq mi.). The total length of coastline is about 3,700 miles. The republic includes many smaller islands, of which the chief are the Wesman Islands (Vestmannaeyjar) off the southern coast, Iceland lies about 520 miles northwest of Scotland and 645 west of Norway." 5 Worldmark encyclopedia, p. 149.

[27] International boundary study, Series A, Limits in the seas, Straight baselines, Ireland, No. 3, issued January 23, 1970.

[28] *Ibid.*, pp. 5 and 7.

[29] See discussion, *supra*, this chapter.

examples of Micronesia and Ireland.[30] The application of the proposal should now be assessed in order to clarify its relationship and limitations in connection with related concerns of the international community.

Before doing so, however, it should be recalled that the purpose of this study was to discuss the law, if any, of *territorial waters* of mid-ocean archipelagos and archipelagic States and to provide a proposed recommendation for the delimitation of *territorial waters* of these mid-ocean archipelagos and archipelagic States. The recommendation would reflect the implications of a concept of symbiosis or a cooperation between States where mutual interdependence was involved. The formula employed within the book was a presentation of the general interests of the maritime nations and the special interests of the archipelagic States. The arguments presented by the authors for justification of the treatment of the archipelagic States as special regimes and the general acquiescence in the force of these arguments and their conclusions was set forth in order to show that, at a minimum, there is now universal acceptance of this premise even among the special and general interest groups as well as the special archipelagic State groups.[31] It must be observed, however, that the polarized positions of these groups has made it impossible for the world community to implement a special regime status into a workable compromise proposal for the delimitation of territorial waters. In other words, there was agreement that these archipelagic States constituted special regimes but nothing concrete could be formulated because of the interests that each group was seeking to protect. The ultimate goal sought to be achieved by this study, therefore, had to be a balancing of these interests in terms of equitable principles *in connection with the delimitation of territorial waters of archipelagic States.* By way of analogy, it was stated that perhaps the proposal could be applied to other mid-ocean archipelagos, as well.

As was mentioned earlier,[32] it is believed that the proposal propounded herein for solving the delimitation problem of territorial waters of archipelagic States gives definable results with a minimum amount of complexity and technical difficulty in the mechanics of the application. Equity is obtained in avoiding arbitrary differences in the application of the proposal among archipelagic States as would certainly continue to occur if the recognition of the special regime status of archipelagic States were to result in a special regime for each of the archipelagic States. The reason for presenting a proposal is the emphatic belief, in this context, that an international law should provide a common formula for all of the archipelagic States rather than special solutions for each one of them. If the development of international law does not take place along the lines of this proposal, it must be recognized that a different solution

[30] *Ibid.*

[31] See text accompanying Chapter IV notes 66–127, *supra.*

[32] See discussion, *supra*, this chapter.

for each archipelagic State may be inevitable. It is to be hoped that such a result does not occur.

A basic premise of this proposal is the belief that the archipelagic States should receive treatment comparable to what coastal or mainland-type States currently enjoy under conventional law in connection with delimitation of territorial waters. At the same time, it is thought that these States should not gain preferential treatment over coastal States because of their particular configurations.

Placed in the territorial waters context of the problem presented in this book, and keeping in mind the fact that any recommendation is to serve as a point of embarkation for universal regulation of delimitation lines regarding territorial waters, it might be well to consider some of the points of criticism that may be expected to be raised in proving out the applicability and effectiveness of the proposal.

To the question of what would be the actual ocean areas that would be obtained by each of the archipelagic States under the *indicator formula*, it is obvious that this is a technical task for cartographers and cannot be attempted herein. The general outline of the result of applying the formula to a number of cases (for example, Indonesia, the Philippines and Fiji) has already been set out.[33]

To the question of what would be the result of applying the *indicator formula* where the breadth of the territorial sea of three, six, nine, or the increasingly accepted 12-mile limit would be extended to 200 miles, so also were a 200-mile economic zone to be adopted, in lieu of, or in order to supplement the existing continental shelf convention, the problem of the actual delimitation of territorial waters of archipelagic States will remain because the archipelagic States will be desirous of having their islands, and the waters lying between, treated as one unit. They have so legislated. This study is focused on the effort to suggest an equitable compromise for the delimitation of territorial waters.

A third question may be posed; namely, that the *indicator formula* is thought to be too mechanical in that it does not differentiate between the treatment of fishing and mineral rights. This criticism suggests that there should be separate territorial water delimitation formulas for fishing rights and for mineral rights. In this setting, it might be argued that the single formula does not give sufficient attention to the socio-economic problems regarding world food production and the international community's interest in conserving fishing stocks at maximum sustainable[34] or maximum economic yields.[35] Regarding mineral

[33] None of these figures (except the distances set forth for Indonesia and the Philippines) was available from The Geographer, U.S. Department of State. See illustrations and discussion, *supra*, this chapter.

[34] Maximum sustainable yield is that amount of fish caught that equals gains to the stock from recruitment and growth minus losses to the stock resulting from natural mortality.

[35] Maximum economic yield is that amount of fish caught (less than maximum sustainable yield) at the cheapest feasible cost. However, the goals of various nations differ. Some states may

rights, as was alluded to earlier in this chapter,[36] it could also be argued that the *indicator formula* for the determination of territorial waters could also be applied to the determination of continental shelf areas. If this were to be done, it would be necessary to establish the machinery to reach agreement between the archipelagic States and the other States regarding the surrendering of excess shelf areas to the international community.

In response to the argument that there should be separate formulas for determining the delimitation of territorial waters with regard to mineral rights, it should be emphasized that it has been demonstrated throughout the manuscript that there is currently no international, customary, treaty law or state practice, regarding mid-ocean archipelagos. The purpose of this study was to set forth and suggest the delimitation of the territorial waters of mid-ocean archipelagos and archipelagic States only. Every author and government recognizes the need for archipelagic States to be treated as a special regime for purposes of delimitation. It was demonstrated that there is universal belief that the special circumstances[37] exist for such a treatment. After all, the basic problem is the need to prepare a basis of discussion for the delimitation of territorial waters of archipelagic States.

Against this background, it is thought that conservation, establishment of a maximum annual catch limit, establishment of quotas, establishment of quotas on different sexes of spawning stock, establishment of rules regarding the prohibition against catching small fish in their larvae and juvenile stages, regulation of gear of the various fleets to selectively harvest larger fish and the prohibition against pollution of spawning grounds in order to maintain or increase a maximum sustainable or economic yield and regulation of fisheries must be done on a world-wide treaty or realistic regional treaty basis, and cannot, in any event, be accomplished on a state-by-state basis.[38]

---

wish to have more fish caught in order to achieve high employment rather than to catch less fish (thereby sustaining and conserving a larger stock) at a cheaper cost. For an example of the very extensive literature in this area, see, *infra*, footnote 38.

[36] See discussion, *supra*, this chapter.

[37] For a discussion of the use of "special circumstances," see *North Sea Continental Shelf* case (1968) I.C.J. Rep. 13–50.

[38] The very extensive literature in this area is found, in general terms, in Francis T. Christy, Jr., Alternative regimes for the marine resources underlying the high seas, 1 Natur. resour. lawyer 63 (1968); F. T. Christy, Jr. and A. Scott, The common wealth in ocean fisheries: some problems of growth and economic allocation (1965); F. T. Christy, Jr., The distribution of the sea's wealth in fisheries, *in* Law of the sea: offshore boundaries and zones (1967); F. T. Christy, Jr., Fisheries and the new conventions on the law of the seas, *in* Law of the sea (1970); F. T. Christy, Jr., Fisheries: common property, open access, and the common heritage, *in* Pacem in Maribus Convocation (1970); F. T. Christy, Jr., Northwest Atlantic Fisheries arrangements: a test of the species approach, 1 Ocean dev. int. law j. 65 (1973); F. T. Christy, Jr., Rules and arrangements for the floor of the ocean: minerals of the deep sea *in* International rules and organization for the sea (1968); James A. Crutchfield, The Convention on Fishing and the Living Resources of the High Seas, 1 Natur. resour. lawyer 115 (1968); J. A. Crutchfield, National quotas for the North Atlantic fisheries: an exercise in second best, *in* Law of the sea: international rules and organization for the sea (1968).

The truth of the matter is that neither fish nor minerals recognize either territorial water boundaries or continental shelf boundaries. Therefore, in order for regulation of fishing and mineral rights to be accomplished, an established set of delimitation rules is needed. That is the first step and it is the purpose of this study to resolve the problem of delimitation of territorial waters of archipelagic States.

If this proposal is acceptable (with appropriate modifications) to the Conference States, the next step is for the Conference States to embody legislative measures in treaty form in order to conserve the world's fisheries. Each State will have to give up something for the common heritage of mankind. This could be done, as Mr. Amerasinghe suggests,[39] by using Hiroshi Kasahara's theory of "preferential rights."[40] However, the problem of conservation of fishing rights on a world-wide basis is an entirely different problem. It is subject to satisfactory solutions only after universal delimitation problems are settled.

In this context, the same reasoning is applicable to the giving up of excess shelf areas for the international benefit of mankind. Again, little progress can be made regarding this matter until universal delimitation problems are resolved. As was stated earlier, there has been a dismal failure with regard to creating uniform territorial sea rights, global fishing regulations and a satisfactory definition of the continental shelf jurisdiction. Every State must have its delimitation problems settled and resolved under uniform international law if fishing and mineral rights are to be satisfactorily dealt with. Otherwise, the States will resent a "what's mine is mine, what's yours we'll compromise" approach to their delimitation problems. Since by their nature, mid-ocean archipelagos are not physically or geographically the same as continental or single island nations, their delimitation problems should be resolved in a uniform manner that is similar to other methods used under conventional law so that they can conform to and receive comparable treatment as continental or single island nations currently enjoy. Only thus may the equities be balanced.

With regard to mineral allocation for the universal benefit of mankind, there is talk of perhaps a levy or tax on certain shelf areas as a possible approach.[41] However, the purpose of this study is to resolve the delimitation problems of territorial waters of archipelagic States and not to attempt to resolve, on a global scale, conservation and regulation of fisheries or exploitation regulation

[39] Mr. Amerasinghe's leading article is: The problem of archipelagoes in the international law of the sea, 23 I.C.L.Q. 539 (Part 3) (1974).

[40] For a further discussion of "preferential rights," see the following articles by Mr. Kasahara: International arrangements for fisheries, *in* Law of the sea: the United Nations and ocean management (1971); International aspects of the exploitation of the living resources of the sea, *in* Pacem in Maribus Convocation, Valletta, 1970 (1971); Problems of allocation as applied to the exploitation of the living resources of the sea, *in* Law of the sea; needs and interests of developing countries (1973).

[41] See Mr. Amerasinghe's article, *op. cit.*, pp. 574–575.

for the common heritage of mankind.[42] Once these special regimes have their delimitation rights resolved, the Conference States can then decide on treaty regulation in order to control the exploitation, development and conservation of the world's natural resources. In doing so, the Conference States will first need to fix the specific goals to be accomplished. However, this, too, is not the subject of this book.

To the question that the proposal of this study does not contribute to the solution of the non-resource uses of the archipelagic waters, the proposal (that is, the *indicator formula*) was intended to eliminate two of the principal problems; namely, the question of the delimitation of territorial waters of archipelagic States regarding fishing rights and mineral rights. As was indicated earlier,[43] the proposal is not directly related to non-resource uses. It is to be emphasized that the reaching of satisfactory formulas for the solution of the two major contentious problems of fishing rights and mineral rights will greatly contribute to the reaching of necessary agreements concerning navigational and other non-resource uses. *Three alternative procedures* have been offered, however, in order to resolve the problem of non-resource uses of the archipelagic waters.[44]

In any case, it is believed that the *indicator formula* proposal for use in connection with the delimitation of territorial waters of archipelagic States (and possibly mid-ocean archipelagos) is thoroughly flexible and could be utilized, hopefully, as a useful basis for discussion. It is further believed that if this proposal were made the basis for specific international conference treaty provisions, it might very well serve to eliminate the threats to international order which the overly persistent reliance upon the traditional terms and concepts has created.

[42] This creation and stabilization of international rules for delimitation of territorial waters appears to be one of the reasons for the sudden desire to create an international ocean agency.

[43] See discussion, *supra*, this chapter.

[44] See discussion, *supra*, this chapter. The second alternative procedure, namely, to provide a uniform distance that would be common to an enjoyment of all the listed non-resource uses, could conceivably eliminate the necessity for expanding territorial waters to an arbitrary length once the fishing and mineral rights of the archipelagic states have been resolved. For a discussion of the necessity of reaching universal accord on the width of the territorial sea, see McDougal and Burke, Public order of the oceans, pp. 446–564.

APPENDIXES

APPENDIX A

"The very excellent research carried on by the International Law Commission and its special Rapporteur on the various aspects of the extent and delimitation of territorial waters has clearly demonstrated the complexity of the problems involved. The practices of and views advocated by coastal States vary infinitely as do the views held by various international authorities and international law publicists.

The legal aspects of the problem are mingled with and dependent upon *various factors of a geographical, economical, historical and political nature. Such factors have lately been increasingly invoked by coastal States for the concrete delimitation of their territorial waters and for the solution of the various other problems concerning the seas adjacent to their coasts.* And, though the broad principles expressed by the International Court of Justice in the Anglo-Norwegian Fisheries Case [footnote omitted] to the effect that:

'The delimitation of sea areas has always an international law aspect: It cannot be dependent merely upon the law of the coastal State as expressed in its municipal law. Although it is true that the act of delimitation is necessarily a unilateral act, because only the coastal State is competent to undertake it, the validity of the delimitation with regard to other States depends upon international law.'

unquestionably give a valid and accurate description of governing legal principles, one must bear in mind that the various factors just mentioned may play an important role in determining the legality under international law of concrete acts of delimitation of territorial waters.

The difficulties in trying to establish a single formula of fixed rules are especially evident where the complex problems concerning the delimitation of the territorial waters of archipelagos are concerned." (Emphasis added.)

APPENDIX A-1

By the terms of that resolution, the General Assembly had conferred to the Conference, as the basis for its proceedings, the draft articles concerning the law of the sea adopted by the ILC at its eighth session. The Official Records of the UN Conference on the Law of the Sea comprise seven volumes: Vol. I: Preparatory documents; II: Plenary meetings; III: First Committee (Territorial sea and contiguous zone); IV: Second Committee (High seas; general regime); V: Third Committee (High seas, fishing; the conservation of living resources); VI: Fourth Committee (Continental shelf); VII: Fifth Committee (The question of free access to the sea of land-locked countries). Volumes III to VII contain the summary records of the meetings and the relevant documents, which appear as indices. These include the draft articles prepared by the ILC and the final texts adopted by the Committee of the Conference. In some areas, the usual replies of the governments to the draft articles submitted by the ILC were notably lacking, especially concerning the subject matter of this thesis. In this connection, Chile stated: "With regard to groups of islands (article 10), a subject on which the Commission was unable to agree, my Government considers that where the islands of an archipelago are separated by narrow passages and surrounded by treacherous waters navigable only by ships of small tonnage, those waters should constitute internal waters." (UN Conf. on L.O.S., Off. rec. vol. I: Preparatory documents, pp. 77–79, at p. 78). The only other reply was made by the representative of Cuba and it stated that "The Government of Cuba regrets that the Commission was unable to formulate a provision concerning the delimitation of the territorial sea around a group of islands or archipelago. The Government of Cuba has taken note of paragraph 4 of the commentary to article 10 of the draft, in which the Commission points out that article 5, concerning straight baselines, may be applicable to groups of islands lying off the coast. It is to be hoped, however, that the Conference will complete the text with a provision envisaging groups of islands pure and simple, and that it will set forth an objective criterion analagous to the one now applicable to offshore archipelagoes. The case for which provision has to be made is that of groups of islands or archipelagoes constituting a single geographical and economic entity; this naturally excludes shoals and islands which, even though forming part of the territory of the State, are widely dispersed and outside the area occupied by the principal group. The latter cases will continue to be governed by the traditional rule, which recognizes that every island has its own territorial sea." *Ibid.*, pp. 79–80, at p. 80.

APPENDIX A-2

The Philippine proposal provided:

"Article 5

1 April 1958

Add a new paragraph, to read as follows:

The method of straight baselines shall also be applied to archipelagos, lying off the coast, whose component parts are sufficiently close to one another to form a compact whole and have been historically considered collectively as a single unit. The baselines shall be drawn along the coast of the outermost islands, following the general configuration of the archipelago. The waters within such baselines shall be considered as internal waters."

"Alternative

Add a new paragraph to article 10, to read as follows:

When islands lying off the coast are sufficiently close to one another as to form a compact whole and have been historically considered collectively as a single unit, they may be taken in their totality and the method of straight baselines provided in article 5 may be applied to determine their territorial sea. The baselines shall be drawn along the coast of the outermost islands, following the general configuration of the group. The waters inside such baselines shall be considered internal waters."

"(If one of these proposals is adopted, the other is automatically withdrawn.)"

Document A/CONF. 13/C. 1/L. 98

The Yugoslavian proposal provided:

"Article 10

26 March 1958

Treat the present text as paragraph 1 and add the following paragraphs 2 and 3:

'The provisions of articles 4 and 5 also apply to islands.' (Paragraph 2.)

'The method referred to in article 5, of straight baselines joining appropriate points on the coast of islands facing the high seas shall be applied in the same way to groups of islands distant from the coast. The areas of sea within such lines and islands shall be considered as internal waters of the islands.' " (Paragraph 3.)

Document A/CONF. 13/C. 1/L. 59.

"Article 5

26 March 1958

Paragraph 3

Delete this paragraph.

Alternative

For the last words of this paragraph, 'have normally been used for international traffic', substitute the following: 'are essential to international traffic using regular sea routes'.

New Article 5A

After article 5 insert a new article worded as follows:

'Waters within the baseline of the territorial sea shall be considered as internal waters.' "

APPENDIX A-3

"28. With regard to paragraph 3 in the Yugoslav proposal, the Yugoslav delegation had originally hoped that the Conference might act on the International Law Commission's recommendation and try to solve the complex and controversial problem of archipelagos. Since that time, however, the only State directly concerned with the problem which had submitted a proposal thereon had withdrawn it, and the Yugoslav delegation would therefore withdraw its own proposal for an additional paragraph 3.

29. Mr. Sorensen (Denmark) regretted the Yugoslav delegation's decision to withdraw its proposal on archipelagos. In its commentary on article 10 the Commission had expressly urged the Conference to give some attention to the problem and an excellent study on the subject had been submitted to the Conference by the Secretariat (A/CONF. 13/18) proposing a solution substantially the same as that advocated by

Yugoslavia. The complexities of the problem would be greatly reduced by the newly adopted text of article 5, which limited the maximum length of a straight baseline to fifteen miles and reserved the right of innocent passage in all areas which a straight baseline would enclose. The Danish delegation would therefore take up the former Yugoslav proposal and formally reintroduced it."

UN Conf. on LOS, Official record, vol. III, p. 162.

APPENDIX A-4

"Frequently the only natural and practical solution is to treat such outlying archipelagos as a whole for the delimitation of territorial waters by drawing straight baselines from the outermost points of the archipelago—that is from the outermost points of the constituent islands, islets and rocks—and by drawing the seaward limit of the belt of marginal seas at a distance of X nautical miles outside and parallel to such baselines. Thus the archipelago viewed as a unit has a continuous area of territorial water. Whether or not an outlying archipelago should be treated in such a manner will, to a large extent, depend on the geographical features of the archipelago. The following criteria may be of importance for the delimitation of territorial waters in any particular case:

(*a*) Though a State in delimiting the territorial waters of its outlying archipelagos must be allowed the latitude necessary in order to be able to adapt its delimitation to practical needs and local requirements, it is equally clear that such delimitation has international law aspects and such aspects may be especially delicate where outlying archipelagos are concerned.

(*b*) In any given case, the more or less close dependence of the territorial sea upon the land domain of the archipelago will always be of paramount importance.

(*c*) The drawing of the baselines must not depart to any appreciable extent from the general direction of the coast of the archipelago viewed as a whole.

(*d*) While the distance between the various islands, islets and rocks of an archipelago obviously may play an important role in the question of whether the drawing of straight baselines is appropriate, no fixed maximum exists as to the length of such baselines. On the other hand it is also obvious that exorbitantly long baselines closing vast areas of sea to free navigation and fishing, are contrary to international law. In such instances there will not be a sufficiently close dependence between the land domain and the water areas concerned.

(*e*) The question as to whether the waters situated between and inside the islands and islets of an archipelago may be considered as internal waters, depends upon whether such water areas are so closely linked to the surrounding land domain of the archipelago as to be treated in much the same manner as the surrounding land.

Each case must be treated on its individual merits in this respect. The geographical configuration of the archipelago concerned will be of primary importance for such determination, though other factors—such as historical and economical factors—may play a role.

(*f*) Even where the waters between and inside the constituent parts of an archipelago are sufficiently closely linked to the land domain to be considered as internal waters, such waters may form a "strait" and consequently be subject to the rules of international law governing "straits" established for the benefit of free navigation and innocent passage of foreign ships."

APPENDIX A-5

For example:
Ecuador, Panama and Peru—"1. The area of sovereignty and jurisdiction of an archipelagic State may be measured from straight baselines joining the outermost points of the outer islands and reefs of the archipelago. 2. In such cases, the waters enclosed by the baselines shall be considered internal waters, though vessels of any flag may sail in them in accordance with the provisions laid down by the archipelagic State." (U.N. Doc. A/AC. 138/SC. II/L. 27.)

People's Republic of China—"An archipelago or an island chain consisting of islands close to each other may be taken as an integral whole in defining the limits of the territorial sea around it." (U.N. Doc. A/AC.138/SC. II/L.34.)

Uruguay—"1. The territorial sea of an archipelagic State whose constituent islands and other natural characteristics form an intrinsic geographical, economic and political entity that has been or may have been historically regarded as such may be measured from the straight baselines joining the furthest points of the islands and the outermost lowtide reefs of the archipelago. 2. Waters enclosed by the baselines drawn in accordance with paragraph 1, irrespective of their depth or distance from the coast, shall be regarded as internal waters without prejudice to the innocent passage of ships flying any flag." (U.N. Doc. A/AC.138/SC. II/L.24.)

Malta—"The jurisdiction of an island State or of an archipelago State may extend to a belt of ocean space adjacent to the coast of the principal island or islands, the breadth of which is 200 nautical miles measured from baselines drawn in accordance with the provisions of Chapter III of this Convention (dealing with the straight baseline system). The principal island or islands of an archipelago State shall be designated by the State concerned and notified to the international ocean space institutions. In the event of disagreement with the designations made by the archipelago State any Contracting State may submit the matter to the International Maritime Court for binding adjudication." (U.N. Doc. A/AC. 138/SC. II/L. 28.) The other proposals submitted did not vary any of the text of the Indonesia, *et al.* proposal. In addition, the other proposals were usually part of broader coverage thus treating the archipelagos, incidentally.

APPENDIX B

"(*i*) the identification of an archipelago for the purpose of the regime is based collectively on geographical, economic, political *and* historic factors;

(*ii*) the straight baseline method as applied between islands may be used for the determination of the base of the territorial sea;

(*iii*) The result of the application of the above method is to establish an outer perimeter from which the territorial sea is determined outward;

(*iv*) there is no maximum limit applicable to such baselines as may be drawn between islands or on the coast of an island nor is there apparently any other limitation, such as reasonableness or alignment with the general direction of the coast or land masses, on the drawing of baselines;

(*v*) there is no limit on the area of waters that may be enclosed within such baselines;

(*vi*) in so far as there is a requirement of political unity it would seem that the limitation is implied that all the islands or land masses between which straight baselines are drawn must belong to a single State.

(*vii*) it does not appear that artificial islands may be used as end-points for baselines, though drying reefs and presumably drying rocks may be so used;

(*viii*) the waters, sea bed, subsoil of the sea within the outer perimeter and the air space above such waters are within the sovereignty of the archipelagic State and are part of the territory of such State;

(*ix*) in spite of (*viii*) above the right of innocent passage is granted to foreign vessels through the waters within the perimeter although this is subject to:

(a) national legislation which should conform to international law;

(b) the right of the archipelagic State at all times to designate sea lanes for such passage;

(*x*) it would seem that foreign States do not have exactly the same right of innocent passage for their vessels as is normally accorded to them through territorial waters but something less than that;

(*xi*) it would seem that foreign States do not have the same right of navigation as they would have through international straits through straits which might previously have been international straits if they lie within the outer perimeter;

(*xii*) foreign States certainly do not have the same rights of navigation as they would have through international straits through the waters as a whole which are within the outer perimeter;

(*xiii*) there are no categories of sea areas within the outer perimeters, such as territorial seas and economic zone [footnote omitted], irrespective of the distance of such areas from the nearest coastline; and

(*xiv*) the sea bed and subsoil within the outer perimeter is totally within the archipelagic State's sovereignty, irrespective of distance from the nearest coastline or depth or whether it is part of the continental shelf."

APPENDIX C

"ARCHIPELAGIC PRINCIPLES AS PROPOSED BY THE DELEGATIONS OF FIJI, INDONESIA, MAURITIUS AND THE PHILIPPINES

Article I

1. These articles apply only to archipelagic States.

2. An archipelagic State is a State constituted wholly or mainly by one or more archipelagos.

3. For the purposes of these articles an archipelago is group of islands and other natural features which are so closely inter-related that the component islands and other natural features form an intrinsic geographical, economic and political entity or which historically have been regarded as such.

Article II

1. An archipelagic State may employ the method of straight baselines joining the outermost points of the outermost islands and drying reefs of the archipelago in drawing the baselines from which the extent of the territorial sea is to be measured.

2. The drawing of such baselines shall not depart to any appreciable extent from the general configuration of the archipelago.

3. Baselines shall not be drawn to and from low-tide elevations unless lighthouses or similar installations which are permanently above sea level have been built on them or where a low-tide elevation is situated wholly or partly at a distance not exceeding the breadth of the territorial sea from the nearest island.

4. The system of straight baselines shall not be applied by an archipelagic State in such a manner as to cut off the territorial sea of another State.

5. The archipelagic State shall clearly indicate its straight baselines on charts to which due publicity shall be given.

Article III

1. The waters enclosed by the baselines, which waters are referred to in these articles as archipelagic waters, regardless of their depth or distance from the coast, belong to and are subject to the sovereignty of the archipelagic State to which they appertain.

2. The sovereignty and rights of the archipelagic State extend to the air space over its archipelagic waters as well as to the water column, the sea-bed and subsoil thereof, and to all of the resources contained therein.

Article IV

Subject to the provisions of Article V, innocent passage of foreign ships shall exist through archipelagic waters.

Article V

1. An archipelagic State may designate sealanes suitable for the safe and expeditious passage of ships through its archipelagic waters and may restrict the innocent passage by foreign ships through those waters to those sealanes.

2. An archipelagic State may, from time to time, after giving due publicity thereto, substitute other sealanes for any sealanes previously designated by it under the provisions of this article.

3. An archipelagic State which designates sealanes under the provisions of this article may also prescribe traffic separation schemes for the passage of foreign ships through those sealanes.

4. In the prescription of traffic separation schemes under the provisions of this article, an archipelagic State shall, *inter alia*, take into consideration:

a. The recommendation or technical advice of competent international organisations;
b. any channels customarily used for international navigation;
c. the special characteristics of particular channels, and
d. the special characteristics of particular ships or their cargoes.

5. An archipelagic State may make laws and regulations, not inconsistent with the provisions of these articles and having regard to other applicable rules of international law, relating to passage through sealanes and traffic separation schemes as designated by the archipelagic State under the provisions of this article, which laws and regulations may be in respect of, *inter alia*, the following:

a. the safety of navigation and the regulation of marine traffic, including ships with special characteristics;
b. the utilisation of, and the prevention of destruction or damage to, facilities and systems of aids to navigation;
c. the prevention of destruction or damage to facilities or installations for the exploration and exploitation of the marine resources, including the resources of the water column, the seabed and subsoil;
d. the prevention of destruction or damage to submarine or aerial cables and pipelines;
e. the preservation of the environment of the archipelagic State and the prevention of pollution thereto;
f. research of marine environment;
g. the prevention of infringement of the customs, fiscal, immigration, quarantine or sanitary regulations of the archipelagic State;
h. the preservation of the peace, good order and security of the archipelagic State.

6. The archipelagic State shall give due publicity to all laws and regulations made

under the provisions of paragraph 5 of this article.

7. Foreign ships exercising innocent passage through those sealanes shall comply with all laws and regulations made under the provisions of this article.

8. If any warship does not comply with the laws and regulations of the archipelagic State concerning passage through any sealane designated by the archipelagic State under the provisions of this article and disregards any request for compliance which is made to it, the archipelagic State may suspend the passage of such warship and require it to leave the archipelagic waters by such route as may be designated by the archipelagic State. In addition to such suspension of passage the archipelagic State may prohibit the passage of that warship through the archipelagic waters for such period as may be determined by the archipelagic State.

9. Subject to the provisions of paragraph 8 of this article, an archipelagic State may not suspend the innocent passage of foreign ships through sealanes designated by it under the provisions of this article, except when essential for the protection of its security, after giving due publicity thereto, and substituting other sealanes for those through which innocent passage has been suspended.

10. An archipelagic State shall clearly demarcate all sealanes designated by it under the provisions of this article and indicate them on charts to which due publicity shall be given."

APPENDIX D

"Article

Rights and obligations of archipelagic States

1. On ratifying or acceding to this Convention, a state may declare itself to be an archipelagic State where:

(a) the land territory of the State is entirely composed of three or more islands; and

(b) it is possible to draw a perimeter, made up of a series of lines or straight baselines, around the outermost points of the outermost islands in such a way that:

(i) no territory belonging to another State lies within the perimeter,

(ii) no baseline is longer than 48 nautical miles, and

(iii) the ratio of the area of the sea to the area of land territory inside the perimeter does not exceed five to one;

Provided that any straight baseline between two points on the same island shall be drawn in conformity with articles . . . of the Convention (on straight baselines).

2. A declaration under paragraph 1 above shall be accompanied by a chart showing the perimeter and a statement certifying the length of each baseline and the ratio of land to sea within the perimeter.

3. Where it is possible to include within a perimeter drawn in conformity with paragraph 1 above only some of the islands belonging to a State, a declaration may be made in respect of those islands. The provisions of this Convention shall apply to the remaining islands in the same way as they apply to the islands of a State which is not an archipelagic State and references in this article to an archipelagic State shall be construed accordingly.

4. The territorial see [Economic Zone] and any continental shelf of an archipelagic State shall extend from the outside of the perimeter in conformity with articles . . . of this Convention.

5. The sovereignty of an archipelagic State extends to the waters inside the perimeter, described as archipelagic waters: this sovereignty is exercised subject to the

provisions of these articles and to other rules of international law.

6. An archipelagic State may draw baselines in conformity with articles . . . (bays) and . . . (river mouths) of this Convention for the purpose of delimiting internal waters.

Provisions

7. Where parts of archipelagic waters have before the date of ratification of this Convention been used as routes for international navigation between one part of the high seas and another part of the high seas or the territorial sea of another State, the provisions of articles . . . of this Convention apply to those routes (as well as to those parts of the territorial sea of the archipelagic State adjacent thereto) as if they were straits. A declaration made under paragraph 1 of this article shall be accompanied by a list of such waters which indicates all the routes used for international navigation, as well as any traffic separation schemes in force in such waters in conformity with articles . . . of this Convention. Such routes may be modified or new routes created only in conformity with articles . . . of this Convention.

8. Within archipelagic waters, other than those referred to in paragraph 7 above, the provisions of articles . . . (innocent passage) apply.

9. In this article, references to an island include a part of an island and reference to the territory of a State includes its territorial sea.

10. The provisions of this article are without prejudice to any rules of this Convention and international law applying to islands forming an archipelago which is not an archipelagic State.

11. The depositary shall notify all States entitled to become a party to this Convention of any declaration made in conformity with this article, including copies of the chart and statement supplied pursuant to paragraph 2 above.

12. Any dispute about the interpretation or application of this article which cannot be settled by negotiations may be submitted by either party to the procedures for the compulsory settlement of disputes contained in articles . . . of this Convention."

APPENDIX E

"79. Concerning archipelagos, reference was made to the question of a special position of archipelagic States in international law and to the various criteria which should determine whether or not groups of islands constituted an archipelago. It was stated that the preservation of the political and economic unity of an archipelagic State and the protection of its security, the preservation of its marine environment and the exploitation of its marine resources justified the inclusion of the waters inside an archipelago under the sovereignty of the archipelagic State or the granting of a special status to such waters. Statements were made regarding passage through archipelagic waters and straits and regarding the nature of such passage. It was also stated that the special status of archipelagic waters was an emerging concept and might be settled as part of an over-all solution of problems relating to the law of the sea.

80. It was also stated that the concept of the archipelagic State was not accepted under existing international law and that if the concept were to be included in a new convention on the law of the sea a precise definition would be needed as well as safeguards for international navigation and a satisfactory procedure for the settlement of disputes. In that connexion it was also stated that the concept of archipelagic waters had grave implications and was unnecessary in that the interests of archipelagic States could be fully covered by the concept of exclusive economic zone or by that of national ocean space. On the other hand, the view was also expressed that the special status of the waters of an archipelago was an existing and accepted concept currently seeking

recognition in a positive and explicit manner as being indispensable to the preservation of the security, integrity and unity of the archipelago. 81. It was stated that some of the rules of the special regime of archipelagic States might be equally applied to the archipelagos that formed integral parts of a State. On the other hand it was noted that such a regime must not be extended to archipelagos which were not archipelagic States.

82. In that connexion it was stated that the regime applicable to the waters contained within a fringe of islands along the coast was clearly established under international law."

APPENDIX F

The representative of the U.S.S.R., Mr. Barabolya:

"*Mr. Barabolya* (Union of Soviet Socialist Republics) said that the question of the legal regime of the waters of archipelagic States, States constituted wholly by one or more archipelagos, was an entirely new problem in international law. There were no special norms in contemporary international law to provide the basis for consideration of that question. All the Committee had before it was proposals from archipelagic and some other States. The question was, however, related to other important questions being considered by the Conference, such as the breadth of the territorial sea and the regime of international straits and economic zones.

The basic principles of contemporary international law provided for the equality of States and mutual respect for the rights of all peoples in the uses of the sea. Yet the concept of a special regime for archipelagic waters meant that there would be different provisions for large areas of ocean between the islands of archipelagic States, which wished to extend their sovereignty over areas of the high seas much larger than their own land area. *Indonesia and the Philippines, for example, claimed sovereignty over an area of the seas almost twice as large as that of their land territory. If the 200-mile economic zone, with the sovereign rights over the living and mineral resources that it implied, was to be added to the archipelagic waters, archipelagic States would have rights over vast areas of the high seas.* (Emphasis added.)

His delegation maintained that the question of the regime of archipelagic waters should be considered together with other related questions. International rules should be drafted to take account of the interests of archipelagic States, which should, however, state clearly and unequivocally that they, in turn, were prepared to be taken into account of the interests of other States. The regime of the waters of archipelagic States should be established in conjunction with a settlement providing for free transit passage along the shortest routes through archipelagic straits and waters traditionally used for international navigation.

In connexion with the question of straight baselines, the length of baselines used to delimit the so-called archipelagic waters and the territorial waters should be limited and clearly defined in the convention. A 48-mile limit had been proposed, but any other reasonable limit could also be considered. It was quite clear that individual islands belonging to archipelagic States should have their own territorial waters and could not be linked to the archipelago by straight baselines. Archipelagic States would, in any case, be in an advantageous position in comparison with other States in respect of living and mineral resources of the sea as they would have rights in a considerably larger part of the seas.

The proposals made by the archipelagic States would be acceptable to his delegation only if they agreed to free transit for all ships through archipelagic straits and waters used for international navigation, and if they recognized the right of unimpeded overflight. Such provisions would not interfere with the right of archipelagic States to use their own archipelagic waters or with their rights over the resources of those waters. He agreed with the representative of Bulgaria that articles 4 and 5 of document A/CONF. 62/C.2/L.49 were unacceptable as they provided only for the principle of innocent passage of ships through archipelagic waters and also because they provided for the possibility of restriction of passage. *Such proposals, which did not strive towards compromise, were unrealistic.* (Emphasis added.) He would be in a position to support the proposals of the archipelagic States if they accepted the 12-mile limit for territorial waters, and free transit, without exception, for ships through archipelagic waters of archipelagic States and through all other international straits."

APPENDIX G

"*Conditions of adjacency.* It is suggested here that some specific limitations to adjacency could be set up in the case of archipelagos; unless such limitations are established and are accepted by a majority of the world's nations almost any situation in which islands, islets, rocks, banks, and shoals are located in some proximity to one another may be considered as meriting a special territorial regime.

According to the proposal outlined here, straight lines up to a maximum of forty nautical miles in length would be permissable between adjacent basepoints; the waters associated with, and enclosed by, these lines, if they are not already within the territorial sea as normally delimited, would be designated as 'insular waters', over which the country would have jurisdiction, subject to certain restrictions. The details of this suggestion are as follows:

1. The straight lines constructed between appropriate base-points within an archipelago are to be known as 'construction lines' to differentiate them from a system of straight baselines.

2. Twelve miles seaward of the construction lines the outer limits of the insular waters will be delimited. All waters within these outer limits, not already included within the traditional twelve-mile territorial limits of the land area, are designated as insular waters . . . . If breaks exist between basepoints which are more than 40 miles in length, they cannot be bridged by construction lines. . . .

3. Insular waters shall have the same juridical status as territorial waters, except that all ships and aircraft in transit shall enjoy the same freedom of navigation and overflight for the purpose of transit through and over such waters, as they have on the high seas. The coastal State may designate corridors suitable for transit by all ships and aircraft through such waters.

4. If, in the case of islands of the archipelago, the coastline is deeply indented and cut into, or if there is a fringe of islands along the coast in its immediate vicinity, the method of straight baselines joining appropriate points may be employed, in accordance with Article 4 of the Geneva Convention on the Territorial Sea and the Contiguous Zone.

5. As regards coral atoll reefs, the edge of the reef as marked on large-scale nautical charts, shall be accepted as the low-water line for measuring the construction line and the territorial sea.

6. With respect to any closed system of construction lines, the total area of insular waters contained within the 12-mile limits calculated from the construction lines may not exceed the aggregate of areas contained within circles 12 miles in radius calculated about each of the basepoints used.

. . .

Rationale for the proposal. The system suggested here is designed to afford archipelago areas an opportunity, under certain prescribed conditions, to assert competence over their inter-island waters. The construction lines are in a sense artificial baselines. From them the seaward limits of insular waters are measured, and all areas of insular waters must be within twenty-four miles of these seaward limits, or the basepoints themselves. Thus, if adjacency in archipelagos can be taken as less than, or equal to, twice the breadth of the territorial sea (measured as twelve miles) then the principle of adjacency is not violated in this proposed scheme.

Waters within twelve miles of the basepoints would be subject only to the normal regime of territorial waters, and not to the additional restrictions of 'insular' regimes, so far as freedom of transit and overflight are concerned. The system suggested here implies also that territorial waters may be delimited in the case of coral reefs, as suggested in the Addendum of the Second Report on the Regime of the Territorial Sea in preparation for the 1958 Geneva Conference. Many of the island groups of the world, such as the Maldives, Truk Islands, and the Palau group have extensive coral formations which themselves form a part of the geographic whole. It would hardly make sense to exclude these features in the delimitation process.

The various restrictions noted here would apply only in the case of delimitations based on the principle of adjacency. If special circumstances exist, either on the ground of history or of economic need, some adjustments in delimitation restrictions may be necessary. There are many situations in which special competence of the coastal country over activities well away from its coast can, in theory at least, be justified. But under no conditions should the freedom of navigation and overflight for purposes of transit, beyond the twelve-mile territorial limits, be compromised Like the regime for straight baselines, this archipelago system should require delineation on officially recognized large-scale charts to which due publicity should be given. . . .

APPENDIX H

"A second possibility woud be to establish a maximum permissible land/water ratio contained within the baselines. In the Norwegian example this ratio is 1:3.5; for archipelagos the limit should be eased to 1:5, because of the basic maritime character of archipelagos. Other examples have been measured from the specific baseline system to determine the following ratios:

Indonesia	1:1
Philippines	1:2.14
Galapagos	1:4.59
Fiji	1:4.88
Tonga	1:25
Bahamas	1:10+
Faeroes	1:3.5

Although 40-nautical-mile 'construction' lines may be drawn, Tonga and the Bahamas could not qualify under this criterion as archipelagos, nor could French Polynesia, the Trust Territory of the Pacific Island, the Cook Islands, and other oceanic atoll groups. The exercise has not been applied to the Maldives, but they probably would not meet the land/water ratio criterion.

iii) *Areal distribution.* If this characteristic has to be quantified, and it may not, one need say only that the maximum transverse axis length must be at least one-tenth of the length of the longitudinal axis. The purpose of this requirement is to prohibit the drawing of archipelago limits around line islands. Such chains of islands—e.g., the Aleutians, Kurils, Lesser Antilles, and Marianas—extend across vast areas of the oceans and seas in narrow chains, often only one-island-wide.

These islands should not be considered as archipelagos. Their problems do not relate to inter-island waters; in fact, the only waters of this nature in the string are situated between two islands. The 12-mile territorial sea accounts for the major problems which are associated with most of these islands. To permit the drawing of construction lines would add little to the economic well-being of the states, for little integration would be gained. The lines, however, would lead to security problems for the world maritime states; each connecting line cuts through a potential strait.

In certain instances, limited problems of these arcuate or line islands may be solved by the 'main-land' concept of straight baselines, i.e., by localized grouping."

APPENDIX H-1

"The Department of State to the American Embassy, Manila, telegram, Jan. 4, 1958, MS. Department of State, file 756D.022/1–458.

It was reported that Senator Arturo M. Tolentino, chief of the Philippine delegation to the Conference on the Law of the Sea held at Geneva in 1960, had informed a news reporter *that no protest was registered by any of the countries represented at the Conference, including the United States, to the Philippine position and that this meant tacit recognition of the Philippine claimed geographical limits.* (Emphasis added.) However, on April 25, 1960, during the course of his address at the Conference, the United States delegate (Dean), as recorded in the Summary Record of the Plenary Meeting held at 9:15 p.m. on that day, stated:

'16. On various occasions speakers had referred to treaties to which the United States was a Party, and had placed interpretations on them at variance with the official United States position and with the facts. Other statements had been made with respect to matters not before the Conference which had been contrary to official United States views. The United States delegation had not considered it necessary or desirable from the standpoint of orderly debate to enter into a discussion of extraneous matters. It merely wished to say that its silence was not to be construed in any way as acquiescence in any views stated at the Conference which were inconsistent with the official position of the United States Government and already made known, in most instances, to the Governments concerned through the diplomatic channel.' "

(The American Ambassador at Manila (Hickerson) to Secretary of State Herter, airgram No. G-195, May 4, 1960, MS. Department of State, file 399.731/5–460; Second United Nations Conference on the Law of the Sea, Summary records of plenary meetings and of meetings of the Committee of the Whole, 17 March–26 April 1960, A/CONF. 19/8, p. 22.)

APPENDIX H-2

"The American Consulate General, Singapore, to the Department of State, despatch No. 326, Jan. 16, 1958, encl., MS. Department of State, file 756D. 022/1–1658; the American Embassy, Djakarta, to the Department of State, despatch No. 328, Jan. 15,

1958, enclosing '*Pengumuman Pemerintah Mengenai Mengenai Wiljah Perairan Negara Republik Indonesia*' ('Government Announcement on the Territorial Waters of the Republic of Indonesia', with official English translation), MS. Department of State, file 399.731/1–1558, encl.; the Department of State to the American Embassy, Djakarta, telegram, Dec. 28, 1957, *ibid.*/12–2857; and the American Embassy, Djakarta, to the Department of State, telegram Dec. 31, 1957, *ibid.*/12–3157. The communique signed at Djakarta, December 13, 1957, is published in the Japanese Annual of International Law, No. 2 (The Japan Branch of the International Law Association, 1958), pp. 218–219.

On January 15, 1958, Australian Minister for External Affairs Casey announced that the Government of Australia had informed the Government of Indonesia that Australia would not recognize or be bound by Indonesia's announced claim to sovereignty over the Java Sea and its superjacent airspace. The American Embassy, Canberra, to the Secretary of State, telegram, Jan. 16, 1958, MS. Department of State, file 756D. 022/1–1658." 4 Whiteman digest of international law, pp. 284–285.

APPENDIX H-3

"I have the honour to refer to Communique issued by the Government of the Republic of Indonesia on December 13th, 1957, claiming that all waters around, between and connecting islands belonging to the Indonesian Archipelago irrespective of their width or dimension from integral parts of inland or national waters subject to the absolute sovereignty of the Republic of Indonesia and also that Indonesian territorial sea shall have a width of twelve nautical miles measured from straight baselines connecting the outermost points of the islands of the Republic of Indonesia, and to state as follows:

The Government of Japan considers that the claims of the Government of the Republic of Indonesia regarding internal waters and territorial sea as stated in the said Communique cannot be admitted under established international law. The Government of Japan, therefore, is unable to recognize the validity of such claims and will not deem them as binding upon its nationals, vessels and aircraft."

APPENDIX I

"The US-administered Trust Territory of the Pacific Islands consists of 2,141 islands and atolls with continued: a total land area of 687 sq. mi. scattered over some 3 million sq. m. of the Western Pacific Ocean, an expanse almost equal to the area of the continental U.S. Only 64 of the islands are regularly inhabited. The territory extends about 1,500 miles from 1° to 20°N. and about 2,700 miles from 130° to 172°E.; its approximate geographical center is the island of Truk, lying about 5,000 miles southwest of San Francisco and 2,000 miles east of the Philippines. Three groups of islands are included in the territory: the Caroline Islands to the south and west, including Palau (188 sq. mi., 7°30′N. and 138°8′E.), Truk (39 sq. mi., 7°25′N. and 151°47′E.), and Ponape (129 sq. mi., 6°55′N. and 158°15′E.); the Marshall Islands to the east, of which Kwajalein (8°43′ to 9°15′N. and 167°30′E.) is the largest atoll; and the Mariana Islands to the north, including Rota (33 sq. mi., 14°7′–12′N. and 145°8–18′E.), Saipan (47 sq. mi., 15°5′–17′N. and 145°41′–50′E.), and Tinian (39 sq. mi., 14°58′N. and 145°38′E.).

. . .

The trust territory is divided into six administrative districts: the Palau, Yap, Truk, and Ponape districts in the Caroline Islands; the Mariana Islands District; and the Marshall Islands District. . . ." Worldmark encyclopedia of the nations 3rd ed., Ed.: M. Y. Sachs (Worldmark Press, Harper and Row, N.Y. 1967), vol. 5.

The Geographer advises that studies are being conducted by their offices with respect to the treatment that the territorial waters of these emerging states shall receive but these studies are not for publication.

BIBLIOGRAPHY

I. PUBLIC DOCUMENTS

A. International

Annuaire de l'institut de droit international, vol. 33, Part 1 (1927).

Annuaire de l'institut de droit international (1928).

Conference for the Codification of International Law, Bases of Discussion, vol. II, Territorial waters (Geneva 1929), League of Nations Doc. C. 74. M. 39, 1929 V.

Evensen, Jens. Certain legal aspects concerning the delimitation of the territorial waters of archipelagoes. United Nations Document A/CONF. 13/18, United Nations Conference on the Law of the Sea, Preparatory documents 1958 (1958), vol. I.

International Law Commission yearbook (1954), vol. II (New York, 1955).

International Law Commission yearbook (1956), vol. I (New York, U.N., 1957).

International Law Commission yearbook (1956), vol. II (New York, U.N., 1957).

United Nations Conference on Law of the Sea, Official records: vols. I–VII (1958) (New York, U.N., 1959).

United Nations. Laws and regulations of the regime of the territorial sea. N.Y., U.N. leg. series, no. ST/LEG/SER. B/6 (1957), vol. 2.

United Nations. Laws and regulations of the regime of the territorial sea. N.Y., U.N. leg. series, no. ST/LEG/SER. B/16 (1974), vol. 2.

United Nations. Report of the Committee on the peaceful uses of the sea-bed and the ocean floor beyond the limits of national jurisdiction. Off. rec.: 28th Sess., G.A. Suppl. no. 21 (A/9021), vols. I–VI (1973) (New York, U.N., 1973).

450 U.N. treaty series 82. Treaty No. I: 6465 (U.N. Doc. A/CONF. 13/L. 53).

499 U.N. treaty series 311. Treaty No. I: 7302 (U.N. Doc. A/CONF. 13/L. 55).

516 U.N. treaty series 205. Treaty No. I: 7477. (U.N. Doc. A/CONF. 13/L. 52).

A. 1. United Nations Documentation from the Third Conference on the Law of the Sea (Caracas, Venezuela, 1974). Not in bound volumes, as yet.

A/CONF. 62/C.2/SR.1 (1st Meeting—organization of work) 8 July 1974.

A/CONF. 62/C.2/SR.2 (2nd Meeting—territorial sea) 11 July 1974.

A/CONF. 62/C.2/SR.3 (3rd Meeting—territorial sea) 17 July 1974.

A/CONF. 62/C.2/SR.4 (4th Meeting—territorial sea) 18 July 1974.

A/CONF. 62/C.2/SR.5 (5th Meeting—territorial sea) 19 July 1974.

A/CONF. 62/C.2/SR.6 (6th Meeting—territorial sea) 22 July 1974.

A/CONF. 62/C.2/SR.8 (8th Meeting—organization of work) 23 July 1974.

A/CONF. 62/C.2/SR.16 (16th Meeting—continental shelf) 30 July 1974.

A/CONF. 62/C.2/SR.17 (17th Meeting—continental shelf) 30 July 1974.

A/CONF. 62/C.2/SR.18 (18th Meeting—continental shelf) 31 July 1974.

A/CONF. 62/C.2/SR.19 (19th Meeting—continental shelf) 1August 1974.

A/CONF. 62/C.2/SR.20 (20th Meeting—continental shelf) 1 August 1974.

A/CONF. 62/C.2/SR.21 (21st Meeting—exclusive economic zone beyond the territorial sea) 5 August 1974.

A/CONF. 62/C.2/SR.22 (22nd Meeting—continental shelf; exclusive economic zone beyond the territorial sea) 5 August 1974.

A/CONF. 62/C.2/SR.23 (23rd Meeting—exclusive economic zone beyond the territorial sea) 6 August 1974.

A/CONF. 62/C.2/SR.24 (24th Meeting—exclusive economic zone beyond the territorial sea) 6 August 1974.

A/CONF. 62/C.2/SR.25 (25th Meeting—exclusive economic zone beyond the territorial sea) 7 August 1974.

A/CONF. 62/C.2/SR.26 (26th Meeting—exclusive economic zone beyond the territorial sea) 7 August 1974.

A/CONF. 62/C.2/SR.27 (27th Meeting—exclusive economic zone beyond the territorial sea) 7 August, 1974.

A/CONF. 62/C.2/SR.28 (28th Meeting—exclusive economic zone beyond the territorial sea) 8 August 1974.

A/CONF. 62/C.2/SR.29 (29th Meeting—exclusive economic zone beyond the territorial sea) 8 August 1974.

A/CONF. 62/C.2/SR.30 (30th Meeting—coastal state preferential rights or other non-exclusive jurisdiction over resources beyond the territorial sea) 9 August 1974.

A/CONF. 62/C.2/SR.31 (31st Meeting—coastal state preferential rights or other non-exclusive jurisdiction over resources beyond the territorial sea; contiguous zone; high seas) 9 August 1974.

A/CONF. 62/C.2/SR.35 (35th Meeting—rights and interests of shelf-locked states and states with narrow shelves or short coastlines; archipelagos) 13 August 1974.

A/CONF. 62/C.2/SR.37 (37th Meeting—archipelagos) 14 August 1974.

A/CONF. 62/C.2/SR.38 (38th Meeting—enclosed and semi-enclosed seas; artificial islands and installations; regime of islands) 15 August 1974.

A/CONF. 62/C.2/SR.39 (39th Meeting—regime of islands) 16 August 1974.

A/CONF. 62/C.2/SR.40 (40th Meeting—regime of islands; transmission from the high seas; other questions) 16 August 1974.

A/CONF. 62/C.2/L.4 (India: territorial sea: nature and characteristics) 9 July 1974.

A/CONF. 62/C.2/L.8. (Turkey: draft article on item 2, territorial sea) 15 July 1974.

A/CONF. 62/C.2/L.10 (Ecuador: proposal on the territorial sea) 16 July 1974.

A/CONF. 62/C.2/L.11 (People's Republic of Bulgaria, *et al.*: draft articles on straits used for international navigation) 17 July 1974.

A/CONF. 62/C.2/L.15 (Denmark and Finland: amendment to draft articles on the territorial sea and straits contained in document A/CONF.62/C.2/L.3) 22 July 1974.

A/CONF. 62/C.2/L.16 (Oman: draft articles on navigation through the territorial sea, including straits used for international navigation) 22 July 1974.

A/CONF. 62/C.2/L.19 (Fiji, draft articles relating to passage through the territorial sea) 23 July 1974.

A/CONF. 62/C.2/L.20 (Algeria: straits used for international navigation: semi-enclosed areas) 23 July 1974.

A/CONF. 62/C.2/L.21/Rev.1 (Nigeria: draft articles on the exclusive economic zone) 5 August 1974.

A/CONF. 62/C.2/L.22 (Greece: draft articles of the Convention) 25 July 1974.

A/CONF. 62/C.2/L.24/Rev.1 (Philippines: historic waters and delimitation of the territorial sea, under items 2.2 and 2.3.2) 19 August 1974.

A/CONF. 62/C.2/L.25 (Greece: draft articles on the continental shelf) 26 July 1974.

A/CONF. 62/C.2/L.26 (People's Republic of Bulgaria, *et al.*: draft articles on the territorial sea) 29 July 1974.

A/CONF. 62/C.2/L.27 (Byelorussian Soviet Socialist Republic, *et al.*: draft article on the contiguous zone) 29 July 1974.

A/CONF. 62/C.2/L.28 (Kenya and Tunisia: draft article on the delimitation of the continental shelf or the exclusive economic zone) 30 July 1974.

A/CONF. 62/C.2/L.30 (Fiji, New Zealand, *et al.*: draft articles on islands and on territories under foreign domination or control) 30 July 1974.

A/CONF. 62/C.2/L.32 (Greece: draft articles on the exclusive economic zone) 31 July 1974.

A/CONF. 62/C.2/L.33 (Austria, Belgium, *et al.*: draft articles on territorial sea) 31 July 1974.

A/CONF. 62/C.2/L.42 (Mexico: draft article on item 5, continental shelf) 6 August 1974.

A/CONF. 62/C.2/L.42/Rev. 1 (Kenya and Mexico: draft article on item 5, continental shelf) 13 August 1974.

A/CONF. 62/C.2/L.43 (Ireland: draft article on delimitation of areas of continental shelf between neighbouring states) 6 August 1974.

A/CONF. 62/C.2/L.44 (Algeria, Bahrain, *et al.*: draft article on definition of straits used for international navigation) 7 August 1974.

A/CONF. 62/C.2/L.47 (U.S.A.: draft articles for a chapter on the economic zone and the continental shelf) 8 August 1974.

A/CONF. 62/C.2/L.50 (Greece: draft articles on the regime of islands) 9 August 1974.

A/CONF. 62/C.2/L.51 (Ecuador: proposal on item 16, archipelagos) 12 August 1974.

A/CONF. 62/C.2/L.52 (People's Republic of Bulgaria, *et al.*: amendments to draft articles on archipelagic States contained in document A/CONF. 62/C.2/L.49) 12 August 1974.

A/CONF. 62/C.2/L.52/Corr.1 (People's Republic of Bulgaria, *et al.*: amendments to draft articles on archipelagic States contained in document A/CONF. 62/C.2/L.49) 26 August 1974.

A/CONF. 62/C.2/L.53 (Romania: definition of and regime applicable to islets and islands similar to islets) 12 August 1974.

A/CONF. 62/C.2/L.54 (Belgium, Denmark, *et al.*: working document on the high seas) 12 August 1974.

A/CONF. 62/C.2/L.55 (Turkey: draft article on item 19, regime of islands) 13 August 1974.

A/CONF. 62/C.2/L.56 (Turkey: draft article on item 17, enclosed and semi-enclosed seas) 13 August 1974.

A/CONF. 62/C.2/L.57/Rev.1 (Australia and New Zealand: draft article on highly migratory species) 22 August 1974.

A/CONF. 62/C.2/L.58 (Argentina, Bolivia, *et al.*: draft article on islands and other territories under colonial domination or foreign occupation) 13 August 1974.

A/CONF. 62/C.2/L.59 (Dominican Republic: draft article on straits and waterways) 14 August 1974.

A/CONF. 62/C.2/L.60 (El Salvador: working paper on item 6, exclusive economic zone) 14 August 1974.

A/CONF. 62/C.2/L.62 (Algeria, Dahomey, *et al.*; draft articles on item 19, regime of islands). 14 August 1974.

A/CONF. 62/C.2/L.63 (Thailand: draft articles on item 16, archipelagoes) 15 August 1974.

A/CONF. 62/C.2/L.64 (Malaysia: amendments to draft articles relating to archipelagic States contained in document A/CONF. 62/C.2/L.49) 16 August 1974.

A/CONF. 62/C.2/L.65 (Bolivia and Paraguay: draft articles on the "regional economic zone") 16 August 1974.

A/CONF. 62/C.2/L.66 (Argentina, Australia, *et al.*: draft article for inclusion in the chapter on the high seas) 16 August 1974.

A/CONF. 62/C.2/L.67 (Indonesia: draft article on historic waters) 16 August 1974.

A/CONF. 62/C.2/L.68 (El Salvador: working paper on the high seas) 19 August 1974.

A/CONF. 62/C.2/L.69 (Fiji, Indonesia, *et al.*: draft article on item 8, high seas) 19 August 1974.

A/CONF. 62/C.2/L.70 (Bahamas: draft articles on archipelagic States) 20 August 1974.

A/CONF. 62/C.2/L.71 (Iraq: draft articles on enclosed and semi-enclosed seas) 21 August 1974.

A/CONF. 62/C.2/L.71/Add 1 (Iraq: draft articles on enclosed and semi-enclosed seas) 22 August 1974.

A/CONF. 62/C.2/L.71/Add 2 (Iraq: draft articles on enclosed and semi-enclosed seas) 26 August 1974.

A/CONF. 62/C.2/L.72 (Iran: draft articles on enclosed and semi-enclosed seas, item 17) 21 August 1974.

A/CONF. 62/C.2/L.72/Corr.1 (Iran: draft articles on enclosed and semi-enclosed seas, item 17) 26 August 1974.

A/CONF. 62/C.2/L.73 (Cuba: amendment to the draft articles on archipelagic States contained in document A/CONF. 62/C.2/L.70) 22 August 1974.

A/CONF. 62/C.2/L.74 (France: draft article on the delimitation of the continental shelf or of the economic zone) 22 August 1974.

A/CONF. 62/C.2/L.75 (Uruguay: draft article on the regime of islands, item 19) 22 August 1974.

A/CONF. 62/C.2/L.76 (Bolivia and Paraguay: equality of treatment in the ports of transit States, item 9.2.2) 23 August 1974.

A/CONF. 62/C.2/L.78 (Egypt, India, *et al.*: draft article on the economic and contiguous zone) 23 August 1974.

A/CONF. 62/C.2/L.79 (U.S.A.: draft article for inclusion in a chapter on the high seas) 23 August 1974.

A/CONF. 62/C.2/L.80 (U.S.A.: draft article for a chapter on the high seas) 23 August 1974.

A/CONF. 62/C.2/L.82 (Ghana, Ivory Coast, *et al.*: draft articles on the exclusive economic zone), 26 August 1974.

A/CONF. 62/C.2/L.83 (Canada, definition of international strait, item 4), 26 August 1974.

A/CONF. 62/C.2/L.84 (Iran: draft article on the continental shelf, item 5), 26 August 1974.

B. National

International boundary study, Series A, Limits in the seas, Straight baselines, Faeroes. Bureau of Intelligence and Research, Office of The Geographer, U.S. Dept of State, Washington, D.C. No. 13, issued March 12, 1970.

International boundary study, Series A, Limits in the seas, Straight baselines, Indonesia. Bureau of Intelligence and Research, Office of The Geographer, U.S. Dept of State, Washington, D.C. No. 35, issued July 20, 1971.

International boundary study, Series A, Limits in the seas, Straight baselines, Ireland. Bureau of Intelligence and Research, Office of The Geographer, U.S. Dept of State, Washington, D.C. No. 3, issued January 23, 1970.

International boundary study, Series A, Limits in the seas, Straight baselines, Mauritius. Bureau of Intelligence and Research, Office of The Geographer, U.S. Dept of State, Washington, D.C. No. 41, issued March 7, 1972.

Islands: normal and special circumstances. The Geographer, Bureau of Intelligence and Research (INR). Washington, D.C., Dept of State, RGES–3, December 10, 1973. 72 p.

Shalowitz, Aaron L. Shore and sea boundaries, with special reference to the interpretation and use of coast and geodetic survey data. Washington, D.C., 1962–1964. 2 v. U.S. Coast and Geodetic Survey, Publication, 10.

Stevenson, John R. Legal regulation of mineral exploitation in the deep sea-bed. 65 Dept State bull. 48, 1971.

————. The search for equity on the seabeds. 64 Dept State bull. 529, 1971.

U.S. Dept of State, Bureau of Intelligence and Research. Islands: normal and special circumstances. Washington, D.C., GPO, 1973. 72 p.

II. TREATISES

A. General

Brownlie, Ian. Principles of public international law. 2d ed. Oxford, Clarendon Pr., 1973.

Hyde, Charles C. International law. 2d ed. vol. I, Boston, 1945.

O'Connell, D. P. International law. 2d ed. London, Stevens & Sons, 1970. 2 vol.

Oppenheim, L. F. L. International law: a treatise, vol. I, Peace, ed. by H. Lauterpacht. 8th ed. N.Y., Longmans, Green, 1955.

Schwarzenberger, Georg. International law. 3rd ed. London, Stevens & Sons, 1957–1968. 2 vol.

Whiteman, Marjorie. Digest of international law. Washington, D.C., GPO, 1963. Vol. 4 (U.S. Dept State, Dept State Publication 7403).

B. Special

Colombos, Constantine J. International law of the sea. 6th rev. ed. New York, D. McKay Co., 1967.

Gidel, Gilbert C. Le droit international public de la mer (The public international law of the sea). La mer territoriale et la zone contigue. 813 p. Chateauroux, Etb. Mellottee, 1932, vol. III.

Grotius, Hugo. The freedom of the seas. Magoffin transl. 1916.

Jessup, Philip C. The law of territorial waters and maritime jurisdiction. New York, G. A. Jennings, 1927. 548 p.

Johnston, Douglas M. International law of fisheries: a framework for policy-oriented inquiries. New Haven and London, Yale U.P., 1965. 554 p.

McDougal, Myres S., and W. T. Burke. The public order of the oceans: a contemporary international law of the sea. New Haven, Conn., Yale U.P., 1962. 1226 p.

Slouka, Zdenek J. International custom and the continental shelf: a study in the dynamics of customary rules of international law. The Hague, Martinus Nijhoff, 1968. 186 p.

Wenk, Edward. The politics of the ocean. Seattle, Washington U.P., 1972. 590 p.

C. Casebooks and Materials

Bishop, Wm. W. Jr. International law cases and materials. 3rd ed. Little, Brown, Boston and Toronto, 1971.

Friedman, Wolfgang G., Oliver J. Lissitzyn and Richard Crawford Pugh. Cases and materials on international law. St. Paul, Minn., West Pub. Co., 1969.

Ordfield, Lester B. and Edward D. Re. International law cases and materials. rev. ed. Indianapolis, Bobbs-Merrill, 1965.

III. ARTICLES

Alexander, Lewis M. Resources of the sea, national jurisdiction and the use of the sea. 8 Natur. resour. j. 373 (1968).

Amerasinghe, C. F. The problem of archipelagoes in the international law of the sea. 23 I.C.L.Q. 539, part 23, 4th ser. (1974).

Anand, R. P. Equitable use and sharing of the common heritage of mankind. *In* L. M. Alexander, ed. Law of the sea: needs and interests of developing countries. Proceedings of the seventh annual Conference of the Law of the Sea Institute, Kingston, R. I., 1972. Kingston, R. I., University of Rhode Island, 1973.

Beesley, J. A. The law of the sea conference: factors behind Canada's stance. Int. perspect. 28–35 (Jul-Aug 1972).

————. Some unresolved issues on the law of the sea. 4 Natur. resour. lawyer 629 (1971).

Boasson, Charles. Resources of the sea and international law. 6 Israel law rev. 291 (1971).

Boggs, S. W. Delimitation of seaward areas under national jurisdiction. 45 Am.J.I.L. (1951).

Bouchez, Leo, J. The concept of effectiveness as applied to territorial sovereignty over sea areas, air space and outer space. 9 Ned. tijdschr int. recht. 151 (1962), no. 3.

————. Some basic problems of coastal state jurisdiction and the future conference on the law of the sea. *In* Annales d'etudes internationales, v. 4, 1973. Geneva, Association des Anciens Etudiants de l'Institute Universitaire de Hautes Etudes Internationales, 1973. pp. 143–170.

Bowett, D. W. The second United Nations Conference on the Law of the Sea. 9 Int. comp. law quart. 415 (1960).

Boyer, A. La Conference de Londres et le droit international de la mer. 16 Droit marit. fr. 515 (1964).

Brantley, Thomas H. Law of the sea. 14 Harvard int. law j. 555 (1973).

Breckner, Norman V. Some dimensions of defense interest in the legal delimitations of the continental shelf. *In* Lewis M. Alexander, ed., Law of the sea: national policy recommendations. Proceedings of the fourth annual conference of the law of the sea institute, Kingston, R. I., 1969. Kingston, R I., University of Rhode Island, 1970. pp. 188/192.

British Institute of International and Comparative Law. Developments in the law of the sea, 1958–64. London, 1965. 208 p. (Its: special publication, 6; international law series, 3.)

Brown, E. D. The 1973 Conference on the Law of the Sea: the consequences of failure to agree. *In* Lewis M. Alexander, ed. Law of the sea: a new Geneva Conference. Proceedings of the sixth annual Conference of the Law of the Sea Institute, Kingston, R. I., 1971. Kingston, R. I., University of Rhode Island, 1972.

————. Our nation and the sea: a comment on the proposed legal-political framework for the development of submarine mineral resources. In Lewis M. Alexander, ed., Law of the sea: national policy recommendations. Proceedings of the fourth annual Conference of the Law of the Sea Institute, Kingston, 1969., Kingston, R. I., University of Rhode Island, 1970. pp. 2–49.

Brownlie, Ian. Recommendations on the limits of the continental shelf and related matters. *In* Lewis M. Alexander, ed., Law of the sea: national policy recommendations. Proceedings of the fourth annual Conference of the Law of the Sea Institute, Kingston, R. I., 1969. Kingston, R. I., University of Rhode Island, 1970. pp. 133–158.

Burke, William T. A negative view of a proposal for United Nations ownership of ocean mineral resources. 1 Natur. resour. lawyer 42 (1968).

————. Ocean sciences, technology and the future international law of the sea. Columbus, Ohio State U.P., 1966. 91 p. (Mershon Centre for Education in National Security, Social Science Program, Pamphlet series, 2.)

————. A report on international legal problems of scientific research in the oceans. Prepared for the National Council on Marine Resources and Engineering Development. Columbus, Ohio, Ohio State U., 1967. 143p.

————. Some thoughts on fisheries and a new conference on the law of the sea. Kingston, R. I., 1971. 17 p. (Law of the Sea Institute, Kingston, R. I., Occasional paper, 9.)

Butler, William E. The Soviet Union and the continental shelf. 63 Am. J.I.L. 103 (1969).

Caflisch, Lucius. The future of the law of the sea. 11 Int. comm. jurists rev. 35 (1973).

Carlson, Sevinc. Soviet policy on the sea-bed and the ocean floor. 1 Syracuse j. int. law com. 104 (1972).

Carter, Jared G. The outlook for the territorial sea and navigation through straits and on the high seas. *In* Marine Technology Society, Law of the sea: reports, 1971. Washington, D.C., 1972. pp. 135–137.

————. The seabed beyond the limits of national jurisdiction. 4 Stanf. j. int. 1 (1969).

Castaneda, Jorge. The concept of patrimonial sea in international law. 12 Indian j. int. law 535 (1972).

Chao, Hick Tin. International fishery regimes and the interests of developing states. *In* Lewis M. Alexander, ed., Law of the sea: needs and interests of the developing countries. Proceedings of the seventh annual Conference of the Law of the Sea Institute, Kingston, R. I., 1972. Kingston, R. I., University of Rhode Island, 1973. pp. 134–139.

Chapman, Wilbert McLeod. Fishery resources in offshore waters. *In* Lewis M. Alexander, ed., Law of the sea: offshore boundaries and zones. Proceedings of the first conference of the Law of the Sea Institute. Columbus, Ohio, Ohio State U.P., 1967. pp. 87–105.

————. The ocean regime of the real world. *In* Lewis M. Alexander, ed., Law of the sea: national policy recommendations. Proceedings of the fourth annual Conference of the Law of the Sea Institute, Kingston, R. I., 1969. Kingston, R. I., U. of R.I., 1970.

————. The theory and practice of international fishery development-management. *In* Law of the sea, v. 7, 1970. San Diego, U. of San Diego School of Law, 1970. pp. 408–454. (San Diego 1. rev. 1970.)

————. The United States fish industry and the 1958 and 1960 United Nations Conferences on the Law of the Sea. *In* Lewis M. Alexander, *ed.*, Law of the sea: international rules and organization for the sea. Proceedings of the third annual Conference of the Law of the Sea Institute, Kingston, R. I., 1968. Kingston, R. I., University of Rhode Island, 1969. pp. 35–63.

Charlier, R. E. Resultats et enseignements des Conferences du droit de la mer (Geneve 1958 et 1960). *In* Annuaire francais de droit international, v. 6, 1960. Paris, Centre National de la Recherche Scientifique, 1961.

Chee, Choung II. National regulation of fisheries in international law. Ann Arbor, Mich., Univ. of Mich., 1966.

Cheek, Conrad H. Law of the sea: effects of varying coastal state controls on marine research, a survey of the U.S. ocean science community. 1 Ocean dev. int. law j. 209 (1973).

Cheever, D. S. Economic development; the great powers and the sea bed. *In* A. Z. Rubinstein and G. Ginzburg, Soviet and American policies in the United Nations. New York, 1971. pp. 95–124.

Cheng, Tao. Communist China and the law of the sea. 63 Am. j. int. 1. 47 (1969).

Christy, Francis T., Jr. Alternative regimes for the marine resources underlying the high seas. 1 Natur. resour. lawyer 63 (1968).

———— The distribution of the sea's wealth in fisheries. *In* Lewis M. Alexander, *ed.*, Law of the sea: offshore boundaries and zones. Proceedings of the first Conference of the Law of the Sea Institute. Columbus, Ohio, Ohio State U.P., 1967. pp. 106–121.

————. Fisheries and the new conventions on the law of the seas. *In* Law of the sea, v. 7, 1970. San Diego, U. of S. D. School of Law, 1970. pp. 455–468. (S.D. 1 rev. 1970.)

————. Fisheries: common property, open access, and the common heritage. *In* Pacem in Maribus Convocation, Valletta, 1970. Pacem in Maribus, v. a: Legal foundations of the ocean regime. Proceedings of the preparatory Conference on the Continental Shelf and Legal Framework, Providence, R. I., 1970. Msida, Royal U. of Malta Press, 1971. pp. 87–111.

————. Northwest Atlantic fisheries arrangements: a test of the species approach. 1 Ocean dev. int. law j. 65 (1973).

————. Rules and arrangements for the floor of the ocean: minerals of the deep sea. *In* Lewis M. Alexander, ed., international rules and organization for the sea. Proceedings of the third annual Conference of the Law of the Sea Institute, Kingston, R. I., 1968. Kingston, R. I., U. of R.I., 1969. pp. 331–333.

Christy, Francis T., Jr., and A. Scott. The common wealth in ocean fisheries: some problems of growth and economic allocation. Baltimore, Md., Johns Hopkins Press for Resources for the Future, 1965. 281 p.

Cisneros, M. The 200 mile limit in the South Pacific: a new position in international law with human and juridical content. *In* Proceedings, American Bar Association, Section of International and Comparative Law, 1964. Chicago, 1965. pp. 56–60.

Clingan, Thomas A., Jr. The continental shelf and the public interest. *In* Lewis M. Alexander, ed., Law of the sea: national policy recommendations. Proceedings of the fourth annual Conference of the Law of the Sea Institute, Kingston, R. I., 1969. Kingston, R. I., U. of R.I., 1970. pp. 193–210.

————. Likely substantive outcome of the next law of the sea conference. *In* Marine Technology Society, Law of the sea: reports, 1971. Washington, D.C., 1972.

————. The oceans. 6 Lawyer Amer. 201 (1974).

————. A second look at United States fisheries management. 9 San Diego law rev. 432 (1972).

————. The transportation industry and the continental shelf. *In* Lewis M. Alexander, ed., Law of the sea: international rules and organization for the sea. Proceedings of the third annual Conference of the Law of the Sea Institute, Kingston, R. I., 1968. Kingston, R. I., U. of R.I., pp. 207–224.

Coquia, Jorge R. The Problem of the territorial waters of archipelagoes, 7 Far Eastern L. Rev. (1959).

Creamer, Robert A. Title to the deep seabed: prospects for the future. 9 Harvard int. law j. 205 (1968).

Crutchfield, James A. The Convention on Fishing and the Living Resources of the High Seas. 1 Natur. resour. lawyer 115 (1968).

————. National quotas for the North Atlantic fisheries: an exercise in second best. *In* Lewis M. Alexander, ed., Law of the sea: international rules and organization for the sea. Proceedings of the third annual Conference of the Law of the Sea Institute, Kingston, R. I., 1968. Kingston, R. I., U. of R.I., 1969. pp. 263–275.

Cundick, Ronald P. High seas intervention: parameters of unilateral action. 10 San Diego law rev. 514 (1973).

Dean, Arthur H. The Law of the Sea Conference 1958–1960. and its aftermath. *In* Lewis M. Alexander, ed., Law of the sea: offshore boundaries and zones. Proceedings of the first Conference on the Law of the Sea Institute. Columbus, Ohio, Ohio State U.P., 1967.

———. The second Geneva Conference on the law of the sea: the fight for freedom of the seas. 54 Am. j. int. Law 751 (1960).

———. The second United Nations Conference on the law of the sea: response. 55 Am. j. int. law 675 (1961).

Delin, Lars. Shall islands be taken into account when drawing the median line according to Art. 6 or the Convention on the Continental Shelf? 41 Nord tidsskr int ret. 205 (1971), no. 1–4.

Dellapenna, J. W. The Philippines territorial water claim in international law. 5 Jour. of law and eco. devel. 45 (1970).

Denorme, Roger. The seaward limit of the continental shelf. *In* Lewis M. Alexander, ed., Law of the sea: national policy recommendations. Proceedings of the fourth annual Conference of the Law of the Sea Institute, Kingston, R. I., 1969. Kingston, R. I., U. of R.I., 1970. pp. 263–274.

Dixit, R. K. Freedom of scientific research in and on the high seas. 11 Indian j. int. law 1 (1971).

Doll, Bernhard. Elements of a regime of the ocean floor. 22 Aussenpolitik (Eng. ed.) 389 (1971), no. 4.

Eichelberger, Clark M. A case for the administration of marine resources underlying the high seas by the United Nations. 1 Natur. resour. lawyer 85 (1968).

———. The seabed question in context: one of the many issues massing for the 1973 conference. 8 San Diego law rev. 653 (1971).

Eisenbud, Robert. Understanding the international fisheries debate. 4 Nat. resour. lawyer 19 (1971).

Ely, Northcutt. American policy in the development of undersea mineral resources. 2 Int. lawyer 215 (1968); 1 Natur. resour. lawyer 91 (1968).

———. A case for the administration of mineral resources underlying the high seas by national interests. 1 Natur. resour. lawyer 78 (1968).

———. Deep sea minerals and American national interests. *In* Lewis M. Alexander, ed., Law of the sea: international rules and organization for the sea. Proceedings of the third annual Conference of the Law of the Sea Institute, Kingston, R. I., 1968. Kingston, R. I., U. of R.I., 1969. pp. 423–430.

———. The laws governing exploitation of the minerals beneath the sea. *In* Exploiting the ocean: transactions of the second annual Marine Technology Society Conference and Exhibit, June 27–29, 1966. Washington, D.C., 1966. pp. 373–378.

———. Seabed boundaries between coastal States: the effect to be given islets as "special circumstances". 6 Int. lawyer 219 (1972).

———. United States seabed minerals policy. 4 Natur. resour. lawyer 597 (1971).

Feliciano, I. P. Comments on territorial waters of archipelagos. 1 Philippine J.I.L. (1962).

Finlay, Luke W. and Maxwell S. McKnight. Law of the sea: its impact on the international energy crisis. 6 Int. J. Georgetown U. Law Center 639 (summer 1974), no. 3.

Fitzmaurice, Sir Gerald. The law and procedure of the international court of justice, 1951–54: points of substantive law—I. 31 Brit. Yb.I.L. 371 (1954).

Francois, J. P. A. La deuxieme conference sur le droit de la mer. 7 Ned tijdschr int. recht 249 (1960), no. 3.

———. Some aspects of the extension of natural sovereignty to adjacent sea. 1 Int. rel. 79 (1955).

Franck, Thomas M., Mohamed El Baradei and George Aron. The new poor: land-locked, shelf-locked and other geographically disadvantaged states. 7 N.Y.U. Jour. Int. Law & Pol. 33 (spring 1974), no. 1.

Franck, Thomas M., Thomas M. Kennedy and Curtis V. Trinko. An equitable regime for seabed and ocean subsoil resources. 4 Denver L. J. 161 (fall 1974) no. 2.

Franssen, Herman T. Developing country views of sea law and marine science. *In* Warren S. Wooster, ed., Freedom of oceanic research: a study conducted by the Center for Marine Affairs of the Scripps Institution of Oceanography, U. of Calif., San Diego. New York, Crane, Russak, 1973. pp. 136–177.

Freeman, Robert O. Possible solutions to the 200-mile territorial limit. 7 Int. lawyer 387 (1973).

Friedmann, Wolfgang. The law of the sea: past, present and future. *In* John J. Logue, ed., The fate of the oceans. Villanova, Pa., Villanova U. P. for the World Order Research Institute, 1972.

———. Selden redivivus—towards a partition of the seas? 65 Am. J.I.L. 757 (1971).

Garcia-Amador, F. V. Latin-America and the law of the sea. *In* Lewis M. Alexander, ed., Law of the sea: a new Geneva conference. Proceedings of the sixth annual Conference of the Law of the Sea Institute, Kingston, R. I., 1971. Kingston, R. I., U. of R.I., 1972.

———. The Latin American contribution to the development of the law of the sea. 68 Am. J.I.L. 33 (1974).

Garcia-Amador y Rodrigues, F. V. Latin America and the law of the sea. Kingston, R. I., 1972. 52p. (Law of the Sea Institute, Kingston, R. I. Occasional paper, 14.)

Goldie, L. F. E. The continental shelf's outer boundary: a postscript. 2 J. marit. law com. 173 (1970).

———. A general international law doctrine for seabed regimes. 7 Int. lawyer 796 (1973).

———. International and domestic managerial regimes for coastal, continental shelf and deep-ocean mining activities. *In* Lewis M. Alexander, ed., Law of the sea: national policy recommendations. Proceedings of the fourth annual Conference of the Law of the Sea Institute, Kingston, R. I., 1969. Kingston, R. I., U. of R.I., 1970. pp. 226–262.

———. The international court of justice's "natural prolongation" and the continental shelf problem of islands. *In* Netherlands yearbook of international law, 1973. Leiden, A. W. Sijthoff, 1973. pp. 237–261.

———. The oceans' resources and international law: possible developments in regional fisheries management. 8 Col. j. transnat. law 1 (1969).

———. Rich and poor countries and the limits of ideology: an introduction to the day's proceedings. 1 Syracuse j. int. law com. 92 (1972).

———. Sedentary fisheries and Article 2(4) of the Convention on the Continental Shelf: a plea for a separate regime. 63 Am. J.I.L. 536 (1969).

———. The United States draft for a United Nations Convention on the International Seabed Area: a "polite conversation". *In* Proceedings of the American Society of International Law at its 65th meeing, 1971. Washington, D.C., 1971. pp. 123–133.

———. Where is the continental shelf's outer boundary? 1 J. marit. law com. 461 (1970).

Gorove, Stephen. The concept of "common heritage of mankind": a political, moral or legal innovation? 9 San Diego law rev. 390 (1972).

Greenwald, Richard J. Problems of legal security of the world hard minerals industry in the international ocean. 4 Natur. resour. lawyer 639 (1971).

Griffin, W. L. Emerging law of ocean space. 1 Int. lawyer 548 (1967).

Grisel, Etienne. The lateral boundaries of the continental shelf and the judgement of the international court of justice in the north sea continental shelf cases. 64 Am. J.I.L. 562 (1970).

Gros Espiell, Hecotr. La mer territoriale dans l'Atlantique Sud-Americain. *In* Annuaire francais de froit international v. 16, 1970. Paris, Centre National de la Recherche Scientifique, 1971. pp. 743–763.

Groustra, Femke. Legal problems of scientific research in the oceans. 1 J. marit. law com. 603 (1970).

Gutteridge, J. A. C. The 1958 Geneva Convention on the Continental Shelf. *In* British yearbook of international law, v. 35, 1959. London, Oxford U.P., 1960. pp. 102–23.

Haight, George Winthrop. Developments in the United Nations relating to sea-bed and ocean floor. 2 Natur. resour. lawyer 119 (1969).

———. Sea-bed discussions in the twenty-fourth General Assembly. 3 Natur. resour. lawyer 405 (1970).

Hanna, Willard A. Nationalizing the Straits of Malacca. Hanover, N. H., 1973. 9 p. (American Universities Field Staff Reports, Southeast Asia series, v. 21, no. 8.)

Hardy, Michael. Offshore development and marine pollution. 1 Ocean dev. int. law j. 239 (1973).

Hargrove, John Lawrence. New concepts in the law of the sea. 1 Ocean dev. int. law j. 5 (1973).

————. A third law of the sea conference: machinery and strategies for reaching agreement. *In* Lewis M. Alexander, ed., Law of the sea: a new Geneva conference. Proceedings of the sixth annual Conference of the Law of the Sea Institute, Kingston, R. I., 1971. Kingston, R. I., U. of R.I., 1972. pp. 147–152.

Harvard Research in International Law. Draft convention on territorial waters, arts. 2–7. 23 Am. J.I.L. (supplement) (1929).

Hayashi, Moritaka. An international machinery for the management of the seabed: birth and growth of the idea. *In* Annales d'etudes internationales, v. 4, 1973. Geneva, Association des anciens etudiants de l'institut universitaire de hautes etudes internationales, 1973. pp. 251–279.

————. Soviet policy on international regulation of high seas fisheries. 5 Cornell int. law j. 131 (1972) no. 2.

Henkin, Louis. Activities of the United Nations General Assembly. *In* Lewis M. Alexander, ed., Law of the sea: the United Nations and ocean management. Proceedings of the fifth annual Conference of the Law of the Sea Institute, Kingston, R. I., 1970. Kingston, R. I., U. of R.I., 1971. pp. 2–22.

————. The extent of the legal continental shelf. *In* Pacem in Maribus Convocation, Valletta, 1970. Pacem in maribus, v. 2: Legal foundations of the ocean regime: Proceedings of the preparatory Conference on the Continental Shelf and Legal Framework, Providence, R. I., 1970. Msida, Royal U. of Malta P., 1971. pp. 15–30.

————. International law and "the interests": the law of the seabed. 63 Am. J.I.L. 504 (1969).

————. Law for the sea's mineral resources. Washington, D.C., 1967. 83 p.

————. The once and the future law of the sea. *In* Wolfgang Friedmann, L. Henkin and O. Lissitzyn, eds. N.Y., Columbia U.P., 1972. pp. 154–170.

Hodgson, Robert D. and L. M. Alexander. Towards an objective analysis of special circumstances: bays, rivers, coastal and oceanic archipelagos and atolls. Kingston, R. I., 1972. 54 p. (Law of the Sea Institute, Kingston, R. I., Occasional Paper, 13.)

Hollick, Ann L. United States oceans politics. 10 San Diego law rev. 467 (1973).

Hull, E. W. Seabrook. The political ocean. 45 For. aff. 492 (1967).

Jain, H. M. Continental shelf—some geological aspects. 12 Indian j. int. law 564 (1972).

Janis, Mark W. The development of European regional law of the sea. 1 Ocean dev. int. law j. 275 (1973).

Jennings, R. Y. A changing international law of the sea. 31 Cambridge law j. 32 (1972).

Jessup, Philip C. The Geneva Conference on the law of the sea: a study in international lawmaking. 52 Am.J.I.L. 730 (1958).

————. The law of the sea around us. 55 Am.J.I.L. 104 (1961).

Johnson, D. H. N. Law of the sea: developments since the Geneva Conferences of 1958 and 1960; Anglo-Scandinavian agreements concerning the territorial sea and fishing limits. 10 Int. comp. law quart. 587 (1961).

Johnson, Ralph W. Fishery developments in the Pacific. *In* British Institute of International and Comparative Law, Developments in the law of the sea, 1958–1964. London, 1965. pp. 133–150.

Johnston, Douglas M. and E. Gold. The economic zone in the law of the sea: survey, analysis and appraisal of current trends. Kingston, R. I., 1973. 53 p. (Law of the Sea Institute, Kingston, R. I. Occasional paper, 17.)

————. Law, technology and the sea. 55 Calif. law rev. 449 (1967).

Joyner, Nancy D. and Christopher C. Joyner. Prescriptive administrative proposal: an international machinery for control of the high seas. 8 Int. lawyer 57 (1974).

Kamenaga, Tomoyoshi. The management of world fisheries. *In* L. M. Alexander, ed., Law of the sea: the future of the sea's resources. Proceedings of the second annual Conference of the Law of the Sea Institute, Kingston, R. I., 1967. Kingston, R. I., U. of R.I., 1968. pp. 122–126.

Kasahara, Hiroshi. International arrangements for fisheries. *In* L. M. Alexander, ed., Law of the sea: the United Nations and ocean management. Proceedings of the fifth annual Conference of the Law of the Sea Institute, Kingston, R. I., 1970. Kingston, R.I., U. of R.I., 1971. pp. 38–42.

————. International aspects of the exploitation of the living resources of the sea. *In* Pacem in Maribus Convocation, Valletta, 1970. Pacem in maribus, v. 3: Planning and development in the oceans. Proceedings of the preparatory Conference on Planning and Development in Relation to Ocean Resources, N.Y., 1970. Msida, Royal U. of Malta P., 1971. pp. 83–90.

————. Problems of allocation as applied to the exploitation of the living resources of the sea. *In* Lewis M. Alexander, ed., Law of the sea: needs and interests of developing countries. Proceedings of the seventh annual Conference of the Law of the Sea Institute, Kingston, R. I., U. of R.I., 1973. pp. 94–101.

Kildow, Judith T. Nature of the present restrictions on oceanic research. *In* Warren S. Wooster, ed., Freedom of oceanic research: a study conducted by the Center for Marine Affairs of the Scripps Institution of Oceanography, U. of Calif., San Diego. New York, Crane, Russak, 1973. pp. 5–28.

Klein, Carl B. The territorial waters of archipelagos. 26 Fed. bar j. 317 (1966).

Knauss, John A. Development of the freedom of scientific research issue of the third law of the sea conference. 1 Ocean dev. int. law j. 93 (1973).

————. Factors influencing a U.S. position in a future law of the sea conference. Kingston, R. I., 1971. 31 p. (Law of the Sea Institute, Kingston, R. I., Occasional paper, 10.)

————. The military role in the ocean and its relation to the law of the sea. *In* Lewis M. Alexander, ed., Law of the sea: a new Geneva conference. Proceedings of the sixth annual Conference of the Law of the Sea Institute, Kingston, R. I., 1971. Kingston, R. I., U. of R.I., 1972. pp. 77–86.

Knight, H. Gary. The draft United Nations Convention on the international seabed area: background, description and some preliminary thoughts. 8 San Diego law rev. 459 (1971).

————. Issues before the third United Nations Conference on the law of the sea. 34 Louisiana law rev. 155 (1974).

Koers, Albert W. Fishery proposals in the United Nations seabed committee: an evaluation. 5 J. marit. law com. 183 (1974).

————. International regulation of marine fisheries: a study of regional fisheries organizations. London, Fishing News Books, 1973. 368p.

Kusumaatmadja, Mochtar. The legal regime or archipelagoes; problems and issues. *In* Lewis M. Alexander, ed., Law of the sea: needs and interests of developing countries. Proceedings of the seventh annual Conference of the Law of the Sea Institute, Kingston, R. I., 1972. Kingston, R. I., U. of R.I., 1973. pp. 166–172.

Langeraar, W. Some thoughts on an international regime and administrating agency for the seabed and ocean floor beyond the limits of national jurisdiction. *In* L. M. Alexander, ed., Law of the sea: national policy recommendations. Proceedings of the fourth annual Conference of the Law of the Sea Institute, Kingston, R. I., 1969. Kingston, R. I., U. of R.I., 1970. pp. 110–119.

Laylin, John G. The law to govern deep sea mining until superseded by international agreement. 6 San Diego law rev. 433 (1969).

————. Past, present and future development of the customary international law of the sea and deep seabed. 5 Int. lawyer 442 (1971).

Leifer, Michael and Dolliver Nelson. Conflict of interest in the Straits of Malacca. 49 Int. aff. (London) 190 (1973).

Levy, Jean-Pierre. La troisieme Conference sur le droit de la mer. *In* Annuaire francais de droit international, v. 17, 1971. Paris, Centre National de la Recherche Scientifique, 1972. pp. 784–832.

Lovald, Johan L. Planning the future of ocean space: a case study of the United Nations Sea-bed Committee 1968–1970. Ann Arbor, Mich., U. Microfilms, 1974. 315 p.

McDougal, M. The law of the high seas in time of peace. 3 Denver j. int. law policy 45 (1973).

————. Revision of the Geneva Conventions on the law of the sea: comments. 1 Natur. resour. lawyer 19 (1968), no. 3.

McDougal, M. and Wm. Burke. The community interest in a narrow territorial sea: inclusive versus exclusive competence over oceans. 45 Cornell law quart. 171 (1970).

————. Crisis in the law of the sea: community perspectives versus national egoism. 67 Yale L. J. (1958).

McKernan, Donald L. A developing policy for international fisheries. *In* L. M. Alexander, ed., Law of the sea: the future of the sea's resources. Proceedings of the second annual Conference of the Law of the Sea Institute, Kingston, R. I., 1967. Kingston, R. I., U. of R.I., 1968. pp. 147–150.

————. International fishery regimes: current and future. *In* L. M. Alexander, ed.,

Law of the sea: national policy recommendations. Proceedings of the fourth annual Conference of the Law of the Sea Institute, Kingston, R. I., 1969. Kingston, R..I., U. of R.I. 1970. pp. 336–344.

Marston, Geoffrey. International law and "mid-ocean" archipelagos. *In* Annales d'études internationales, v. 4, 1973. Geneva, Association des anciens etudiants de l'institut universitaire de hautes études internationales, 1973. pp. 171–190.

Martinez, Arthur D. The politics of territorial waters: 12 miles or 200? 8 Stud. comp. int. dev. 213 (1973).

Mendoza, Estelito P. The base-lines of the Philippine archipelago. 46 Philippine law j. 628 (1971).

Miller, H. Crane. Ocean dumping—prelude and fugue. 5 J. marit. law com. 51 (1973).

Miron, George. The outer continental shelf: managing (or mismanaging) its resources. 2 J. marit. law com. 267 (1971).

Misra, K. P. Territorial sea and India. 6 Indian j. int. law 465 (1966).

Moore, Jonathan R. The future of scientific research in contiguous resource zones: legal aspects. 13 Indian j. int. law 231 (1973).

Murty, B. S. The international regulation of the uses of the sea-bed and ocean floor. 9 Indian J. int. law 72 (1969).

Nawaz, M. K. Alternative criteria for delimiting the continental shelf. 13 Indian J. int. law 25 (1973).

————. Chinese views on the law of the sea: select aspects. 12 Indian j. int. law 606 (1972).

Nelson, L. D. M. The patrimonial sea. 22 Int. comp. law quart. 668 (1973).

Nordquist, Myron. The legal status of Articles 1–3 of the Continental Shelf Convention according to the north sea cases. 1 Calif. west. int. law j. 60 (1970).

Nordquist, Myron and Amanda Lee Moore. Emerging law of the sea: issues in the Mariana Islands. 7 J. int. law econ. 43 (1972).

O'Connell, D. P. The juridical nature of the territorial sea. 45 British year-book of international law 303 (1973).

————. Mid-ocean archipelagos in international law. 45 British year-book of international law 1 (1973).

Oda, Shigeru. New developments in the United Nations Sea-bed Committee. 4 J. marit. law com. 577 (1973).

————. Proposals for revising the convention on the continental shelf. 7 Columbia j. transnat. law 1 (1968).

————. Towards a new regime for ocean development. 1 Ocean dev. int. law 291 (1973).

Onorato, William T. Apportionment of an international common petroleum deposit. 17 Int. comp. law quart. 85 (1968).

Opoku, Kwame. The law of the sea and the developing countries. 51 Rev. droit int. 28 (1973).

Oxman, Bernard H. and John R. Stevenson. The preparations for the Law of the Sea Conference. 68 Am.J.I.L. 1 (1974).

Palmer, William. The United States draft United Nations Convention on the international sea-bed area and the accommodation of ocean uses. 1 Syracuse j. int. law com. 110 (1972).

Pardo, Arvid. Development of ocean space: an international dilemma. 31 Louisiana law rev. 45 (1970).

Park, Choon-Ho. Oil under troubled waters: the Northeast Asia sea-bed controversy. 14 Harvard int. law j. 212 (1973).

Pearson, Charles S. Extracting rent from ocean resources: discussion of a neglected source. 1 Ocean dev. int. law j. 221 (1973).

Petaccio, Victor. Water pollution and the future law of the sea. 21 Int. comp. law quart. 15 (1972).

Pharand, Donat. Historic waters in international law with special reference to the Arctic. 21 Univ. Toronto law j. 1 (1971), no. 1.

Pinto, Christopher W. Problems of developing states and their effects on decisions on law of the sea. *In* Lewis M. Alexander, ed., Law of the sea: needs and interests of developing countries. Proceedings of the seventh annual Conference of the Law of the Sea Institute, Kingston, R. I., 1972. Kingston, R. I., U. of R.I., 1973. pp. 3–13.

Pollock, Howard W. Fisheries considerations of ocean space. 4 Natur. resour. lawyer 676 (1971).

Pratt, Wallace E. Petroleum on continental shelves. 31 Bull. Amer. Assn. Petroleum Geologists 658 (1947).

Rao, K. Krishna. The legal regime of the sea-bed and ocean floor. 9 Indian j. int. law 1 (1969).

Ratiner, Leigh S. National security interests in ocean space. 4 Natur. resour. lawyer 582 (1971).

————. United States oceans policy; an analysis. 2 J. marit. law com. 225 (1971).

Reeves, Jesse S. The codification of the law of territorial waters. 24 Am.J.I.L. 486 (1930).

Riphagen, W. International legal aspects of artificial islands. 4 Int. relat. (London) 327 (1973).

Robertson, J. W. Security interests and regimes of the sea. *In* Lewis M. Alexander, ed., Law of the sea: the future of the sea's resources. Proceedings of the second annual Conference of the Law of the Sea Institute, Kingston, R. I., 1967. Kingston, R. I., U. of R.I., 1968. pp. 47–51.

Schram, Gunnar G. International fishery regimes and the interests of coastal states. *In* Lewis M. Alexander, ed., Law of the sea: needs and interests of developing countries. Proceedings of the seventh annual Conference of the Law of the Sea Institute, Kingston, R.I., 1972. Kingston, R.I., U. of R.I., 1973. pp. 130–133.

Slouka, Zdenek J. United Nations and the deep ocean: from data to norms. 1 Syracuse j. int. law com. 61 (1972).

Sorenson, Max. The territorial sea of archipelagoes. 6 Neth. Tidsk. int. recht 315 (1959).

Stevenson, John R. The United States proposal for legal regulation of seabed mineral exploitation beyond national jurisdiction. 4 Nat. resour. lawyer 571 (1971).

Syatauw, J. J. G. Revisiting "the archipelago": an old concept gains new respectability. 29 India quart. 104 (1973).

———. Some newly established Asian States and the development of international law. The Hague, M. Nijhoff, 1961. 249 p.

TABLE OF CASES

INDEX

GPSR Compliance

The European Union's (EU) General Product Safety Regulation (GPSR) is a set of rules that requires consumer products to be safe and our obligations to ensure this.

If you have any concerns about our products, you can contact us on ProductSafety@springernature.com

In case Publisher is established outside the EU, the EU authorized representative is:

Springer Nature Customer Service Center GmbH
Europaplatz 3
69115 Heidelberg, Germany

Batch number: 10830943

Printed by Printforce, the Netherlands